THE SECRET LIFE
OF FUNGI

THE
SECRET LIFE
OF FUNGI

DISCOVERIES FROM A HIDDEN WORLD

ALIYA WHITELY

PEGASUS BOOKS
NEW YORK LONDON

THE SECRET LIFE OF FUNGI

Pegasus Books, Ltd.
148 West 37th Street, 13th Floor
New York, NY 10018

ISBN: 978-1-64313-785-8

10 9 8 7 6 5 4 3 2 1

Printed in the United States of America
Distributed by Simon & Schuster
www.pegasusbooks.com

For my father

Contents

Introduction

We were always walking.

We walked along the Devon coast, or in the woods, as soon as my legs were long and strong enough to take me. My father always had his camera. He wanted to capture something of the bright sights we saw: painted fishing boats jostling in the harbour; the vivid, flashing feathers of the robin or the blue tit; or the tall wildflowers of the open fields, campion pink and poppy red, and the buttercup's shining face turned up to the sun.

I preferred Exmoor after the rain: damp, dank browns, slabs of stone, and old, twisted tree trunks. The strange shapes that sprang on them, around them, between them.

When I was first given my own camera I was delighted, but I soon discovered I had no skill for it. I hadn't yet developed a sense of what makes a good photograph. I wasn't drawn to the things that adults learn to appreciate as beautiful, or eye-catching. Instead I tried to capture the essence of the moor, snapping the rocks, the trees, the tough grasses and the suspicious sheep. And I remember I took photos of fungi, small and slimy, or scattered over rotting wood. I had been given one inviolable command – *don't touch* – but I loved to look at them.

They were not a pretty view. They were something else. They could be flat and smooth, almost shiny, or creased in texture, like folded paper. They could look bold, defiant, in the way their caps reared up from their stems, or they could be a mess of rotting material from which insects crawled and snails oozed.

I posted my first rolls of film at the local shop and waited for the photographs to be developed and returned. I remember my excitement, and my disappointment, when I opened the envelope and discovered I'd captured only blurred, indistinguishable images. There was some secret to that world that could not be caught on camera – at least, not by me. Still, I kept trying. I wanted to understand it.

I wonder, now, how much understanding springs from connection. It's not possible to know a subject truly without seeing where it touches other fields of knowledge. Back then, I hadn't even realised that what I was photographing, searching out, were often mushrooms. Mushrooms, to me, came in punnets and could be found on 1970s supermarket shelves. They were called buttons: small, neat, in their place. The stems held specks of dirt. They had erupted from the soil; I knew that much. But I made no link between them and the bulbous growths on the trunks, or the pointed caps amid the dead leaves.

But then, we live in a world of connections we don't quite make. The roads cover the continents and plane trails criss-cross the sky. The internet creates incredible opportunities for communication, for togetherness, and yet there is such loneliness in the 7 billion of us. But we are all intimately linked, part of this one world, and fungi is one of the strongest glues that binds us. They can appear anywhere, from desert dunes to frozen tundra, and create anew from rotting matter. They can invade bodies and thoughts, and they can live under our feet or on them, between our toes or between our floorboards. They are unwelcome intruders or vastly expensive treats. Fungi are a diverse and difficult group to classify. At first naturalists thought they were sponges, or some other form of animal, possibly even worms. Often they were categorised as strange, unsettling plants. It has taken

hundreds of years to reach the modern scientific definition, and study continues to bring new information to
light. There's still so much to learn about these secretive
forms of life, including the tantalising question of how
much they communicate with each other, and with many
other organisms. Perhaps they are even trying to communicate with us.

The mushrooms I used to find on the moor were part
of fungi that grew in darkness. They wound their way
through the soil and found, in the earth, roots and bulbs
and larvae and bacteria and life and death in many forms.
I've been fascinated by this for many years, and I'm still
taking my snapshots and trying to find out more than a
handful of their secrets. I keep making small connections
across fields of knowledge: geography, history, myth and
fiction, science and culture. For each one I've written
about in this book there could be so many more; there
are countless connections to make.

Fungi are not like us – they are entirely, magically,
something else. This is a glimpse into their incredible,
surprising and dark secrets, and an insight into the secret
fungal world: the eruption, growth and decay overhead,
inside us and under our feet.

ERUPT

1

To Name, To Know

It's the size of a saucer, with a pale, brownish cap, and an earthy smell that wafts up from where it sits in its soil-filled cardboard box. My friend and I, side by side, peek over the lip of the box and stare at it.

There's a sense of the forbidden about being in this corner of the science classroom before the bell has even gone, but when we heard there was a poisonous killer thing placed next to the fume cupboard we had to come and see for ourselves. This doesn't look like a killer. It's not an object I can identify from theory, although I know what it is in a general fashion, of course. I ask the question anyway: *What is it?*

It's just a mushroom.

Biology is not my best subject. I can never seem to make the leap from the page to the body. We don't get to do many practical lessons in my school, but watching the teacher slice up an eye, earlier that term, has confused me. The leaking fluids obscured the textbook view, and the spongy quality of the eye under the knife left me squirming.

This mushroom is a corporeal object too, reminding me of that eye. It has a coarse, almost scaly texture to its flat cap, and the smell of it is strong, emanating from the box as if it is growing as we watch – an active aroma of climbing damp and shifting soil. I tell my friend she's wrong. It can't be just a mushroom. It's something else. There should be a giant, impressive word for this squatting beast. I try on 'toadstool', but that doesn't seem right either. I'm reaching at the limits of my language; I can't explain it to her, and we fall out over this semantic difference, and don't speak for weeks.

We were both wrong, and we were both right.

It was just a mushroom. Looking back at it now, I'm fairly certain it was *Agaricus campestris* – a Field Mushroom.

I don't know what it was doing in the corner of the class-room. Perhaps it had been brought in as a project, or found by the teacher, and the size and smell of it worked its magic on a class of bored and impressionable students looking for an element of interest, maybe even danger. Stories about it spread as quickly and easily as spores: mushrooms can commandeer our imaginations. Maybe it's just as wise to say: a mushroom is never just a mushroom, and it is never wise to take any of them for granted.

It sparked something in me. I wanted to have the language to name it, to know it. Still, it took a while for that desire to erupt, to find its way to the surface. I was studying at university (not biology – that eye put paid to any such ambitions for me) when I got around to buying a book on the subject. It was called *Field Guide to Mushrooms of Britain and Europe* and it described the Field Mushroom as edible, and fairly common. The book also informed me that it can be mistaken for *Amanita phalloides*, the Death Cap, which contains over twenty poisonous compounds and is famously fatal to humans. Another reason never to take a mushroom for granted.

The *Field Guide to Mushrooms of Britain and Europe*, written by H. and R. Grünert, contained wonderfully vivid, intense photographs that revealed how different mushrooms could be. They ranged from the morels, with their scrunched, spongy textures, to the domed, comforting pillows of the boletes. There were puffballs: fleshy, swollen lumps as big as a cow's head in one picture, and their apparent opposites, growing outwards in firm yet delicate flat discs: the brackets. Gill fungi looked fanned and velvety, rich ruffled material beneath their caps, and who could fail to be intrigued by the phalloids, tall and sticky, or curling over into strange, almost floral growths? And yet these photographs came with a warning in the introduction: never become complacent about identification. No number of pictures, illustrated or photographed, can capture every aspect of a mushroom. Even the most experienced foragers need to double-check, to be certain. The book told me not to rely on the visual, but to read the descriptions carefully and take my time.

Even the most standardised description of a mushroom contains an element of stylistic evocation that's difficult to describe. They are such potent, sarcous objects that bringing them into sharp focus with words takes skill: a level of skill that could be found in my new field guide. Along with the descriptions came the English language names, beyond the drier, scientific Latin. They had a resonance of their own, from Bog Bell to Fairy Sparkler, passing through Rubber Ear and Dead Man's Fingers along the way.

Who gave mushrooms these wonderful titles? Many come from traditional British folk names, which means some mushrooms have had many different ones over the years. Identification guides published over the last three centuries or so have added their own, often without much success in getting them to stick. The process of streamlining to one accepted name has yet to end. My 1992 edition of the field guide had many as-yet-unnamed entries. But there has been a more recent push to give each Latin name an English counterpart. The British Mycological Society formed a working party in 2005 to give us more common names for fungi; their website lists them, as currently agreed on, and also includes a list of protocols to follow to suggest new ones. Could all mushrooms get their own names? That seems unlikely – there are over 15,000 species of wild mushrooms in the UK alone. But it would be good to have more words, if only to keep up with the more generously named wild flowers of Britain.

The word 'toadstool' came to me when I looked at that large flat mushroom, but my instinct that it was not a good fit was both correct and incorrect. The words 'mushroom' and 'toadstool' are pretty much interchangeable, although some of us tend to think of toadstools as the poisonous varieties of mushroom. It's a great word though, conjuring images of a warty toad squatting atop a slimy, dank growth. Perhaps the venomous nature of toads led to the association – there's no evidence to suggest toads do like hopping about in highly fungal areas, although both like the damp, I suppose. The word dates back to the Middle Ages.

That one unnamed, indescribable mushroom-not-mushroom started me thinking, and challenged my language. I'm still trying to come up with new ways to bring them to life on the page today, as my chances to spot them in the wild diminish. The Field Mushroom, then: let's start there. When's the last time you saw one, erupted from the earth and swelling to the size of a saucer? I might phone my old friend and ask her if she wants to go looking for one with me. Let's all go on a long walk and replace words with experience. Let's go now.

2

A Small Field

I could start the business of describing a mushroom with talk of gills, flesh and cap. Or I could mention the way it springs up from underground, or the spores it creates that get taken on the breeze. The smell, the texture, the environment in which it can be found: all of these are ways to get to know these fruiting bodies a little better.

I'll start with an easy mushroom to picture: something like the Shaggy Inkcap (*Coprinus comatus*), squatting happily amid the blades of grass in a small green field not far from here. The Inkcap is a friendly sight: a whitish woolly cylinder that opens into a bell-shaped cap to look so like our shared idea of what a mushroom is that describing it feels a little redundant. So how will I delineate it from all the other mushrooms of this book, and the world?

I need professional help – the services of a taxonomist.

Taxonomy is a branch of science that, at first, sounds as if it lacks the scope of the great big umbrella subjects of biology or chemistry. But the science of naming and categorising organisms encompasses all of our understanding; it attempts to make sense of everything we think we know so far. Without it there's no order. Taxonomic systems exist for arts and sciences, the law and for the military, for computing and economics, education, health . . . and mushrooms, of course. Not just mushrooms. All fungi.

The father of modern taxonomy: that's an impressive label, and it belongs to Carl Linnaeus, the eighteenth-century botanist and zoologist who spent decades finding and examining plants, animals and minerals in his efforts to understand how they all fit together. He invented the system of classification the scientific community still uses today by creating a nested hierarchy based on the shared characteristics of groups. So much of our information has changed, grown, since Linnaeus first set up his system. Still the approach, in essence, remains the same, as does the business of naming each sample. The two-part Latin name you find next to any common name (they are scattered throughout this book from *Agaricus campestris* onwards) comes from Linnaeus: a formal system known as binomial nomenclature. Our Shaggy Inkcap's Latin name, when translated, tells us quite a bit of handy information about it: *Coprinus* means 'living on dung' and *comatus* means 'hairy'. It certainly makes it easier to picture this particular mushroom.

A good place to start trying to make sense of what fungus is might be with Linnaeus – what did he make of it? I can feel better about my own problems in this area when it comes to understanding this strange form of life; Linnaeus didn't know what it was either. He thought fungi might be a type of plant, or that they might even belong to the animal kingdom after he observed 'thousands of little worms' in dried fungi placed under a microscope. It turns out that fungi belong in neither category, but to a different kind of life altogether – a third kingdom, that can live in symbiosis with, or parasitically on, both plants and animals in ways we are still uncovering.

We may make our own boundaries around our knowledge, but it will continue to expand. As we'll learn later, it's in the nature of fungi to be intimately connected with every other form of life and our understanding of how that works might change again. But, at least for now, here are some basic definitions that give the study of mycology some kind of shape.

Fungi are organisms that digest animal and plant material through a process called osmotrophy – invading the material and sending out enzymes to break down substances into sugars, fatty acids, amino acids and so on. The cell walls of fungi are made of glucans and chitin: glucans can be found in plants, and chitin is a hard, semi-transparent material (otherwise found in the exoskeletons of insects, crustaceans and spiders) but only fungi combine them. Many types of fungi produce spores, and they can reproduce sexually or asexually. They are more closely related to animals than plants.

What types of organism might we expect to find in the field of fungi? Mushrooms, of course. They are the fruiting bodies that grow from mycelia, which is the collection of threadlike matter called hyphae. Mushrooms dominate our idea of what fungus looks like, swelling up in the right conditions to take us by surprise with their vivid colours and varied shapes. They can be tiny or enormous, fleshy or firm or gelatinous. Or as perfectly photogenic as our Shaggy Inkcap.

And there are yeasts, being put to work by humanity for thousands of years in breweries and bakeries to make bread rise and sugar ferment – although there are many more types of yeast in the wild, living on fruits and plants, even on and inside animals. Including humans, of course.

We see moulds regularly too, often with displeasure registering in our expressions. Although yeasts are single-celled organisms, moulds are formed by hyphae creating a fuzzy network that can feed on, say, rotting fruit. Think of the thick, dusty blue-green coating that thrives on the orange you forgot in your fruit bowl. That's probably *Penicillium digitatum*, a mould that is ruthlessly effective at colonising small cuts and bruises on harvested fruit.

Smut fungi are probably less in our thoughts on a daily basis, but they are multicellular organisms that live alongside us in a different way, on our agricultural crops such as oats, sugarcane, wheat and maize, sometimes destroying the plants in the process. And parasitic rust fungi infect plants too, often leaving a powdery coating on their victims. A rose infected by a common rust, say, such as *Phragmidium*, can be marred by the orange spots on its withering leaves.

Lichen are a little different, and fascinating for it – composite organisms that include algae or bacteria alongside fungi, living mutually, growing in practically every environment around the world. And beyond that there are the mind-blowing amounts of fungi that we can't even see, from chytrids to microsporidia, often evolved to live in incredibly specific host environments. For instance, *Loma salmonae* is a fungal parasite that infects only the Pacific salmon, causing disease in the gills and shortened lifespans.

These all seem a long way away from the Shaggy Inkcap we're looking at amid the long green blades of grass, but they are all part of the same form of life. This one little hairy mushroom on a pile of dung links to them, and belongs in their number.

Maybe there's no such thing as a small field. As soon as you start to look more closely at what's around you, it becomes clear that there's so much to take in, both in taxonomical and mycological terms.

So, after hundreds of years of study, we continue to examine fungi closely, and find them in so many other fields too – in trying to understand allergies or agriculture, medicine and microbiology, and climate, cuisine and culture. One field of study informs another; under the surface, they are all connected.

Whatever fungi are, they are everywhere.

3

The Common Mushroom

Buy it as a Button if it's young and white, neat and closed. Buy it as a Chestnut if it's young and brown, earthy and pert. Buy it as a Portobello if it's mature and open, the cap large, the gills visible. In the end, it's all the same mushroom, no matter what it's called on the packaging. You might also find it described as Swiss Brown, Italian Brown, cultivated or table, but its proper name is *Agaricus bisporus*: the Common Mushroom.

It's the most widely cultivated, bought and sold mushroom in the Western world, and it has provided many of us with our archetypal fungal smell-and-taste experience – pleasant, firm, good in a stew or sliced and fried, or maybe dotted in an omelette. When there are so many different fungal flavours to try it's perhaps surprising that we've opted for this one as our favourite, but perhaps that says more about ingrained fears of the unknown, particularly when it comes to eating more adventurous varieties. The evolution of humanity has certainly depended on our ability to resist the temptation to pop anything that looks interesting into our mouths for a chew. We have good reason to be wary of mushrooms we don't immediately recognise.

Having said that, humanity does have a long history of finding and enjoying edible fungi, dating back at least 19,000 years to a cave burial in El Mirón, northern Spain. The recent discovery of a woman's skeleton, painted in red ochre and laid to rest, enabled scientists to examine her dental enamel and ascertain that bolete mushrooms were very possibly part of her diet. I'd guess she wasn't on the adventurous side when it came to choosing her fungi, following tried-and-tested advice passed down to her.

But still, there are a million mushroom recipes to try, even if you go no further than *Agaricus bisporus*. Versatility might well be the reason for the success of the Common Mushroom – that, and the ease with which they can be grown en masse, industrially, using a process that has been perfected. It starts in a bed of straw and shit, thick with bacteria: a different kind of recipe yielding results quickly as shelves of mycelia obediently begin to produce their fruiting bodies.

The benefit is that the common mushroom will reproduce asexually. Each is a clone of the last. Eventually this could cause its own problems; the threat becomes pest resistance when so little diversity exists within the market. This is a problem we see in the banana business, where the sweet variety Cavendish dominates our supermarket shelves. Ironically, Cavendish is susceptible to a particular fungal disease called fusarium wilt, which spreads easily through the genetically identical plants and has nearly wiped out the banana trade in the past. Sexual reproduction ensures a healthy mix of genetic material that enables organisms to develop their own defence mechanisms to new threats, but it does lead to more mutations – and we do love our dependable, identical *Agaricus bisporus*.

But, for now, the Button/Chestnut/Portobello industry continues to yield magnificent, mushrooming results. No matter how they're labelled, pick some up and give my recipe a go before you start to think of them as common rather than widespread. I promise you, it's delicious.

Slow Mushroom Stew with Cheese Dumplings

Start with lots of *Agaricus bisporus*, any strain, any level of maturity. You'll also need an onion and some garlic, half a bottle of red wine, a tin of chopped tomatoes, a spoonful of redcurrant jelly and a handful of thyme.

Chop the onion and garlic, and quarter the mushrooms, then fry them for a few minutes. Then pour in the wine and tomatoes, add the jelly and the thyme, and throw the whole lot in the slow cooker for the day.

An hour before serving, make your dumplings by rubbing together some self-raising flour and a bit of butter before stirring in lots of cheese – any kind as long as it's strong (I prefer Cheddar) – and mixing them into a dough using a few tablespoons of milk. Roll out the dough and cut rounds, then put them over the top of the mushroom mixture for the final 40 minutes or so, until they are risen. Make sure you get a bit of sauce and bit of dumpling with a good, firm, quartered Common Mushroom in every mouthful. A rare treat.

4

Forays and Feasts

There's elegance to the foray, as a word, as an idea. *Foraging* has a more active, rooting sound, suiting its meaning: the acquisition of food by hunting, fishing, gathering plants. Or mushrooms, of course. But the walk itself, the slow searching out of the fungi in a woodland stroll, say, or over wet green hills on an overcast afternoon, is given a genteel quality by being classed as a *foray*.

The first use of the word in the context of a fungal discovery mission comes from the English county of

Herefordshire, and the Woolhope Naturalists' Field Club. The Woolhope still exists today; it has been a regular gathering of those interested in the natural world for over 150 years. In the second half of the nineteenth century, at a time when richer Victorians were developing curiosities and collective instincts when it came to the changing world around them, the very first 'Foray Among the Funguses' was held. The year was 1868, and notable early mycologists gathered to go foraging together. I can't tell you what they found on that first stroll. I wonder if *Coprinellus disseminatus* was among their finds – the Fairy Inkcap, hanging like little grey bells in great number from rotting wood, a friendly and pleasant sight for any forager. Or perhaps they came across *Mucilago crustacea*, expressively known as Dog Sick Slime Mould, which is an off-white pile of unpleasantness from a distance that reveals an intricate, loose and foamy structure if you can bear to get closer. Both of these types of fungi have been spotted in recent years by the Herefordshire Fungus Survey Group, according to their website; it's wonderful to think they are species that might have been there from that first foray until now, just waiting to be found and re-found by every adventurous party.

I can tell you that whatever they found (that was edible, of course) they picked and brought back to the Mitre Hotel in Hereford, where they had a feast. They ate well. One of their number, an illustrator and architect called Worthington George Smith, designed a beautiful menu card, and the whole event was such a success that it was repeated the following year, and the next, and the next, until it became an annual event that was much anticipated by the group. The menu cards became collectible items, and it's not hard to see why; one from an event at the Green Dragon Hotel in 1877 is covered in entertaining and elaborate illustrations, featuring smiling edible mushrooms, and grinning skulls for the poisonous varieties. There are also bottles of wine and crossed cutlery decorating the borders of a magnificent five-course menu. The options for diners included a range of meats and fish, and desserts including a vanilla cream. 'Bifteck' was also on the menu – not a meat, but *Fistulina hepatica*, a bracket fungus also known as Beefsteak Polypore, which can be used as a meat substitute. The 'Bœuf salé' (corned beef) was served with the 'Woolhope Club sauce' – could that have been made from the results of their own forays on the day? I hope so.

It all sounds like the kind of event that would appeal now as much as then; don't we, once more, live in a time of renewed interest in the natural world, and our changing place within it? Perhaps that's why the British Mycological Society (formed in 1896 from the Yorkshire Naturalists' Union, another strong force in maintaining interest and pride in local wildlife) holds a UK Fungus Day. It's held annually on 3 October, and features events across the country such as organised walks, talks, and activities such as photography competitions. A foray sounds like an ideal way to celebrate the occasion – a sedate and gentle stroll to find fungi, to see them squatting on tree trunks, or to find them freshly risen on a damp day in their honour. There's no compunction to pick them and eat them. Just to see. And then home for a feast – or, at least, a meal with a possible side order of Woolhope sauce. Given the lack of a recipe, I'll make something up. After all, traditions can be upheld in spirit and energy, even if they must be remade for each age.

5

Learn, Carry, Collect

In September 1991 a man emerged from a glacier.

The ice mummy was named Ötzi after the location in which he was found: the Ötztal Alps, a mountain range that in part forms the border between Austria and Italy. At first he was thought to be a modern man, perhaps a dead mountaineer, but dating revealed him to be Europe's oldest mummy, frozen in the ice over 5,000 years ago.

Ötzi was a Chalcolithic traveller, from what is called the Copper Age. He was possibly a shepherd, his bodily proportions revealing he had walked long and far over hills for much of his life. He carried everything he needed to survive with him, and those objects reveal much about him.

He wore shoes and a cloak. He carried an axe, made of a copper blade tied by a leather strip to a wooden handle, and he also had a dagger and part of a bow. On his back was a large pannier made from hazel rods and twisted grass cords. A container made of birch-tree bark was among his possessions, as was a disc of white marble attached to strips of fur, from which he probably hung the dead birds he had hunted.

And he carried two types of fungi.

Fomes fomentarius is also known as Hoof Fungus, or Tinder Bracket. The fruiting bodies form on some types of tree – often birch, beech or sycamore in the UK – and do look surprisingly hooflike: protruding from broken bark, they are curved, usually dark in colour, and form a strong, hardening crust. Although they can smell almost fruity, they're inedible, but Ötzi had some in his possession for the many miles he walked.

If it's not good to eat, why carry it? It turns out that the name, Tinder Bracket, holds the answer. Archaeologists studying Neolithic fire-lighting techniques found that the inner part of *Fomes fomentarius*, dried and ground, creates a substance that might well have been a key part of Ötzi's fire-lighting kit, carried in a pouch around his waist.

There were also two pieces of Birch Polypore, *Fomitopsis betulina*, found in Ötzi's possession. They had been threaded on to hide strips, which were probably tied to his wrist. He kept them close; perhaps they were precious to him. Birch Polypore is a bracket fungus, forming only on damaged birch trees. It's a thick wedge of rubber to look at, turning from a creamy white to grey-brown as it ages, and it has a pleasant smell of the kind associated with many fungi: that of the soil, and of yeasty, damp growth. It is edible, but apparently the taste is not pleasant.

Another common name for the Birch Polypore is the Razor Strop; it's possible Ötzi used it to hone the blades of his axe and dagger, running their edges over the fungus. It's fascinating to think that these common names could reflect a truth so old, crossing histories and societies.

Another possibility, dating back through the centuries: a shared belief in the medicinal properties of tree fungus. Studies of *Fomitopsis betulina* have shown that it contains agaric acid, which can cause bouts of diarrhoea. Linked with the antibiotic properties of the fungus, and the discovery that Ötzi suffered from whipworm, an internal parasite that might well have caused him ongoing stomach pains and anaemia, could it be that he was carrying his own medical supplies?

Medicinal mushrooms are an idea that can be found throughout history, from Ötzi onwards. Hippocrates wrote of the anti-inflammatory benefits of certain fungi circa 400 BCE, and Chinese practitioners of traditional medicine have been using mushrooms for centuries. Many peoples have their own knowledge about the fungal world and its curative capabilities – for instance, Australian Aboriginal lore has included information, passed orally through the generations, about fungi that has barely been recorded in written form. But in this new age of the Anthropocene we store much of our knowledge away in devices, not holding it in our heads. Instead we learn when and where to access it, and then we forget about it until the next time it's needed. Why keep it close? One search, one word, and it will be back in front of our faces again. Numbers and addresses, maps and meanings and more.

For a long time, the world was not this way, and the only knowledge you had was the kind you could carry on your body, or in your head.

From the Alps to Ancient Greece, from the vast-
ness of China to the outback of Australia, fungi have
had their uses beyond food and flavour. And they still
do now. These uses are known to many, passed between
them on their travels. What great and mighty networks
of knowledge we have always created, and continue to
create, finding new answers and uncovering old ones.
Thoughts from yesterday and today, combining to make
new thoughts for tomorrow.

6

Saviours

I have an app on my phone for positive news, and it gives me daily reports of progress, of happiness, to counterbalance that tangled knot of tensions that live in my throat. But sometimes it's difficult to believe in these little snapshots of simplified science, easy-reading events. I wish I had more faith in the idea that a certain discovery could solve just one of our problems, and maybe even save millions of lives, or the planet, in the process. On the bad days, I shake my head at that two-paragraph tale of a far-fetched fungus that could eat all pollution or cure a terrible disease, and I swipe onwards. Back to the bad-news apps; they're much easier to keep faith with.

But why shouldn't a fungus save millions of human lives? It's done it before. The discovery of penicillin deserves to headline a collection of humanity's most happy accidents. Alexander Fleming left his laboratory in 1928 to take a holiday. He returned to find his Petri dishes had been contaminated with a greenish mould – *Penicillium notatum* – and that mould was happily killing the bacteria that had been in those samples.

If this sounds too simplistic a breakdown of the past, you're right, it is. From that starting point the business of getting to the first antibiotic relied on the skill, ingenuity and determination of people in fields from chemistry to biology to crystallography to logistics and the hundreds of others that never usually get a mention. Does that mean the information is untrustworthy? I suppose it means that we should learn to look more closely, and with sharper eyes, to see the difference between the events that are being simplified and the events that are being built up to more than a sum of their parts to make us believe in them – good or bad.

In the past few years there have been numerous reports of plastic-eating fungi, discovered in places from the Amazonian rainforest to a rubbish dump in Pakistan, and we love them for the possibilities they offer. A few broad strokes of the pen paint a picture of a better world, achieved with the minimum of fuss, and the fungus itself barely gets a mention. It falls into that category of things we don't need to understand, and that's true – we don't need to understand the *Penicillium* genus of fungi to appreciate antibiotics. But I find I want to know the organisms lurking behind the news: not to comprehend them, or to make a judgement about their efficacy (which would take years of study even to approach as a possibility), but simply because they're the little source of hope at the centre of these stories.

The *Aspergillus* mould genus, a microfungi, can be found pretty much everywhere, and seen nowhere, unless you have a microscope to reveal them as puffy yellow discs dotted randomly on a dark background. Living in damp conditions or in air-conditioning, they can be the cause of serious disease and affect the breathing in immuno-compromised people. But they are widespread throughout nature, and the more we search for them, the more we find them. Who knows how many kinds there are? In 2017 alone thirty-seven more species were found, and there are many that we already make use of in processes as diverse as cotton processing, soft-drink manufacturing, and the treatment of multiple sclerosis.

Aspergillus tubingensis was discovered in 1934, but it was only in 2017 that a team of scientists began to suspect that it could have huge environmental benefits when it was found feeding on polyurethane on a rubbish site at Islamabad. It breaks down plastic material by secreting enzymes and using mycelia to break apart molecules of polymers at an astonishing rate, shrinking the usual time of decomposition from years to weeks. This microfungus might provide a way to conquer the profusion of plastics that is overtaking our world, on land and at sea; tests have shown it responds to changes in climate and situation, showing different results according to soil temperature and acidity levels, and so work continues to track down the best way to harness its particular skills for our benefit.

The same can be said of *Pestalotiopsis microspora*. Under a microscope it resembles a white-green lozenge with horizontal black lines and a small white stubby tail. It is not a new discovery; it was first catalogued by a mycologist in 1880. But a team of Yale molecular biophysics and biochemistry undergraduates took a trip to the Amazon rainforest in 2011 and identified the ability of this fungus to feed on polyurethane. It has attracted keen scientific interest since.

Pestalotiopsis microspora is an endophyte: an organism that lives within a plant, to the benefit of both. Incredibly, this fungus has the unique capacity to live exclusively on polyurethane in anaerobic conditions. It could survive deep in the darkness of landfill and steadily work its way through many kinds of plastic, if initial hypotheses turn out to be accurate. These complex relationships are everywhere, and they offer potential benefits in many other chemical, pharmaceutical and biofuel advances.

There's a tipping point where it doesn't matter whether you gain hope from these discoveries or not. There's only the reality, and belief is an irrelevance. Because of that, it's very easy to take penicillin for granted – and other everyday fungal miracles inspired by Fleming's discovery. His work was a key factor in the decision of a young Japanese biochemist called Akira Endo to investigate the effect of certain fungal enzymes on cholesterol. Endo found that *Penicillium citrinum* could change synthesis levels of cholesterol in the blood, and this starting point led to the eventual creation of one of the most commonly taken drugs in the world: statins.

So if, one day, I find it commonplace that there are vast man-managed plains of fungi treating our ailments and eating up the landfill we left behind, I'll still have other problems to untangle from that knot in my throat, and maybe I'll despair of those instead. I suspect that's the way the human race moves forward: trying to untangle those knots and forgetting the ones they've straightened along the way.

But if it does happen in my lifetime, I hope I'll remember to find wonder in it. In the meantime, I want to take time over the short paragraphs that make up the good news, to remind myself that sometimes solutions do exist. And I'll hold onto this: Fleming found a fungus that saved millions of people and inspired other scientists to find their own solutions, and there's no reason why bad news is better than good.

7
Fruiting Cities

A night rain falls, and the world turns to a quiet morning. Outside my bedroom window, the view of the lawn has been transformed: mushrooms, squatting and settled on the stretch of grass as if they've always been there. They are speedy, sure invaders.

They haven't grown overnight. They haven't grown in the traditional sense at all; instead, their cells have absorbed water, expanded and elongated, creating a force that drives them upwards at speed. Mushrooms are simply the fruiting bodies of some fungi. The ones asserting themselves confidently on my lawn are, I think, *Marasmius oreades*, known as Scotch Bonnets, or Fairy Ring Champignons. They are pale brown, yellowish, with wide flat tops, and they appear in circles, radiating outwards from some mysterious central point beneath the ground. I could eat them – but I'm not confident enough in my identification to risk it. They're easy to confuse with other, deadly varieties such as *Clitocybe rivulosa* – Fool's Funnel, which also can appear in rings. Best left alone, and silently viewed from above on this still, new autumn day.

Underground, woven through the soil of my lawn, there's a network of microscopic threads called hyphae. These form the mycelium – the vegetative part of the fungus, growing and finding nutrition. It needs no sunlight to survive, even thrive. Nourishment comes from the digestion of animal and plant material, and when compatible hyphae meet, and mate, a mushroom is produced.

Then it waits for the right conditions. It monitors temperature and moisture levels: a mushroom is 90 per cent water. The rain is a call to swell. Here it comes, fast and robust. The world looks different in a matter of hours.

The English philosopher and social reformer Jeremy Bentham wrote in 1787, 'Sheffield is an old oak;

Birmingham but a mushroom.' At that time Birmingham was in the grip of a revolution. It had erupted in industry, technology, philosophy; it was the hub of what became known as the Midlands Enlightenment. Did Bentham think it would shrink away as quickly as it had sprung into being? Perhaps not. He continued, 'What if we should find the mushroom still vaster and more vigorous than the oak?'

Oaks can stand tall for hundreds of years, but many types of fungus can harm them, infiltrating their bark, stealing their nutrients. Some share a mycorrhiza – a symbiotic relationship between plant and fungus. These friendships can start well, with a beneficial exchange. The tree and fungus trade food, even information, but later the fungus can switch to parasitic behaviour. We don't know why the sudden change of heart; as ever, fungi retain their secrets.

Can a fungus be vaster and more vigorous than an oak? Can a city of mycelium compete with a city of wood, or even stone?

Picture a city of the future, created from mycelium. Dried blocks of fungus form the bricks of structures as tall and strong as oak, stretching to the sky. Architects and artists have been expanding this vision for decades, creating installations and companies that explore the possibilities of mycelium construction.

Mycelium bricks are low-carbon and easy to make. They have benefits as building material, including being fire-resistant and termite-proof. To create the bricks, spores are fed on sawdust and sugarcane until a spongy mass forms, which is transferred into a mould and then dehydrated. The combination of ingenious architecture and a knowledge of fungi is leading to exciting ventures. In 2014 the Museum of Modern Art in New York City showcased *The Living*: a collection of mycelium bricks, highlighting them as 'a new vision for our society's approach to physical objects and the built environment through living structures that respond to current crises of material sustainability'.

We've grown further still. In 2017 architect Dirk Hebel and engineer Philippe Block created Mycotree, a branching structure made from compressed mycelium bricks that can support itself, and even provide the framework of a two-storey building. It is stunning to look at. As beautiful as a tree, of course – like living under the branches of a forest. An organic creation that offers the hope of producing architecture that comes from, and returns to, the earth.

But to concentrate only on the sudden fruiting cities of the future is to miss what lies here in the present.

In the Southern Highlands of New South Wales, Australia, lies a disused railway tunnel, once a major engineering feat that an expanding population outgrew. Now it's the home of a cultivated mushroom farm. Since 1987 Li-Sun Mushrooms has been carefully encouraging exotic varieties such as enoki and shimejii– it's the only farm in Australia to grow them. Enoki are bunched pinpoints of white, crisp and long-stemmed, much used in Japanese cuisine. Shimejii are fatter, rounder, also growing in bunches from a single point. They are both delicate mushrooms that thrive on damp logs, cool air, little light: the depths of our own discarded networks make a good home for them. They are happy to live in absolute dark; the only light needed in these locations is for human eyes, when we come to harvest the fruiting bodies. Other mushroom growers around the world have used caves, or miles of limestone tunnels from mining operations, or even an abandoned water park. Fungi, in one form or another, can grow nearly anywhere.

Fungi farming is also integrating directly into city resources, finding its niche within our existing urban systems. In 2019, Netherlands-based company Rotterzwam opened a mushroom nursery in Rotterdam that converts 6,000 to 7,000 kilos of used coffee grounds from the city into 1,200 to 1,400 kilos of oyster mushrooms, *Pleurotus*, every month. A crowdfunded project, the nursery uses solar power, and then returns the processed substrate to the soil after harvesting; the nursery should be carbon-negative within a matter of years. Their plans are free to all who might want to create such businesses for themselves. Mark Slegers, co-founder of Rotterzwam, says, 'The goal is to have a facility in every city.'

Mushrooms grown from our discarded produce, housed in structures grown from mycelium: this is a picture of a symbiotic relationship between human and fungus to create the fruiting cities of our future. Perhaps both humanity and fungi can be vigorous and vast, and yet able to last. We wake up to a view of a new world that is erupting around us, over us. We are part of it. It looks strong.

8

Weak Seeds Need Strong Friends

Fungi of so many kinds are living close by, in the fields and forests around us, and although some can be destructive, many are not. A number form a mycorrhizal association: a symbiotic relationship with a variety of surrounding plants enabling the exchange of nutrients through their mycelial network – the threads of hyphae that branch out and grow from their tips, searching for new partners.

Mycorrhizae (from the Greek, meaning 'fungus' and 'root') occur all the time, everywhere, between so many plants and fungi that it would be ridiculous even to attempt to list them. They can be mutualistic or parasitic relationships, or they can change between the two. They can be complex and fascinating – challenging human ideas of individuality, of what a lone organism is – once we begin to understand the levels of exchange that are taking place. We tend to interpret these exchanges as gifts or as trades: *that's yours, now this is mine.*

In the case of orchids this exchange starts, as so many things do, as a seed.

The seed is so small – it can be less than a millimetre in length – and it's not strong. Unlike other seeds, the orchid seed contains no energy and cannot grow on its own. It would become something beautiful, given the chance, but it needs a friend to find it.

The hyphae of a fungus come across it, and the mycelial network gives the small seed what it wants: energy. The seed sucks up what it is given, and it germinates. It begins the process of growing.

This is not an unusual exchange. This is the way all orchids begin. There are over 25,000 species of orchids and all of them are dependent on fungi at some point in their life cycle. Even after they are fully grown, orchids might still retain that mycorrhizal relationship, although many become capable of getting energy directly from the sun, using photosynthesis.

I've seen wonderful photos and drawings of orchids, but I can't recall ever seeing one in the wild, not in the way I've come across mushrooms. Do they really have the delicate, intricate grace that the image gives them? Drawn, in particular, they look to me like a complex schematic made by a master draughtsman. Constructed in reality, would a slow breath out dismantle them, lay them bare to their component parts? I wonder if I'd see the fungus there, wrapped up in its relationship at the roots, feeding the flower. An illustration of an orchid without a fungus friend is missing a key part. They cannot be truly understood without each other.

For instance: *Epigogium aphyllum*. The ghost orchid. (Not to be confused with *Dendrophylax lindenii*, also known as the ghost orchid, which is found only in Florida and Cuba.) It has the distinctive, intricate shape of any orchid, and its splayed petals are greyish white, so thin they seem translucent, half-hiding in the dark. There are some pale-pink markings too: sparse blushes. It has been described as a rarest plant in the UK, and has yet to be cultivated because of the necessity of its extremely complex symbiosis with *basidiomycete* fungi – that is, fungi such as puffballs, brackets, boletes, jellies, chanterelles, smuts, rusts and others; this is a diverse group – which is, in turn, forming mycorrhizae with certain trees. Barely anyone, anywhere, has seen a ghost orchid. If I ever did get lucky enough to set eyes on one, I would really be looking at not one relationship, but many. This particular orchid gets *all* its energy from fungi, sometimes from different kinds of fungi simultaneously. It never even begins to turn to the sun. No photosynthesis here. It relies utterly on its underground friends: the unseen, unsung fungi.

Forgive me if this is a romantic vision. Orchids seem to have that effect on people. But since finding out that they are essentially reliant on fungi, I have a new perspective. They are not lone, rising, random gifts, like treasure. They are weak and desperate, and they are gamblers, hoping their luck holds and a good strong friend can be found close by to give them everything they lack.

What do the fungi get out of the deal? The relationship of the orchid to the fungus is described as myco-heterotrophic, with the plant sometimes viewed as a sort of parasite, taking the carbon it needs and giving nothing back. Perhaps there's more we need to learn here, to understand it fully. But, for now, I'll anthropomorphise and romanticise it further by maintaining that a fungus can make a really good friend, especially if you're a rare, weak seed with no energy of your own.

9

Cryptic Clues

Lost in the business of trying to understand an academic article, I find myself absorbed in the pleasing art of finding satisfying words to say aloud – and noting that many of them can be found amid fungus. Is there a word for this hobby? A quick online search reveals lists of words that people love to say, from onomatopoeic ones to good old profanities. There are also the ones many people hate to say out loud, such as 'moist', to which you could also make a tenuous fungal connection.

Yes, my mind is wandering off the page.

Never mind the science. I'll keep finding good words to say. Like today's winner on the page: 'zoospore'. I could say 'zoospore' all day. It's a swimming spore, and it's not the product of the fungal kingdom alone. Some bacteria and eukaryotic (containing cells with a nucleus) organisms also use zoospores to reproduce. Looking at an illustration of one, it would be easy to think it resembles a sperm, with its round body and long, thin tail, which is called a flagellum. Flagellum: there's another satisfying word to say, and there are more coming.

Zoospores are a method of asexual reproduction used by aquatic fungi such as chytrids, which you might spot infecting your pet goldfish or reptile. My interest today, and the academic article I'm attempting to decipher, deals with *cryptomycota* – fungal microbes that, as the name might suggest, remain much of a mystery.

Cryptomycota (say it, let it roll around on the tongue) were discovered only in 2011, not because they're 'new' in any sense of the word, but because of our improving ability to see and understand microscopic worlds. They're a strange and diverse group of fungi, found in ponds, seas, chlorinated water, any water, and there is a conundrum at the heart of their discovery. They appear to lack a characteristic that was part of the definition of a fungus: the use of chitin in their cell walls. Chitin helps to form a tough, rigid structure, allowing organisms to keep their forms even against tremendous pressure. Could *crypto-mycota* really be fungi without it?

Our answer comes from the very cutting edge of science. RNA sequencing – determining the patterns of certain molecules in ribonucleic acid – shows that these organisms really are fungi, and there's so much more work to do, study to be undertaken.

Things change; knowledge changes, from the microscope to genetics, and levels of cytological study that reveal the answers to so many puzzles. As yet, we know very little about this form of life. But new knowledge will erupt, and will connect previously separate things in strange ways, and then the act of translating that knowledge, passing it down through words, will begin. One day, children will read about it in textbooks, and the facts laid out before them will make a straight line from the once cryptic clues that scientists managed to solve. How easy it might seem in retrospect, looking back at the path of knowledge found, painstakingly picked out along the way.

Like many of us, I'm not able to decipher the science at these levels, but I'm in love with the words. Is it enough to know that mycology is still growing and changing, and to wonder where the words will take us next? Meanwhile, the moist zoospores of the *cryptomycota* swim on.

10

Blanket Coverage

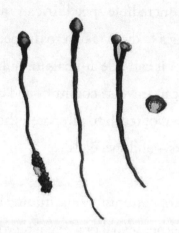

A spore is a microscopic message: a blueprint of reproduction. It's not a developing embryo, unlike a seed. It contains only one cell. When it is released – perhaps from the gills of its mushroom, or ejected at force due to the build-up of fluid pressure inside its fungus, say – it is one of thousands, even millions, but that doesn't mean its message is unimportant. It might be the one spore that lands in the perfect place, wherever may be right for it to start the next stage of its life. It will lay the groundwork for more of its kind, and more, to continue the industry of survival, to start the cycle again.

A spore is a daredevil. It can be a bold glider, a champion swimmer or a living cannonball, flung upwards, outwards, at incredible speed. It can tame insects to its will, infecting a body to take it to the perfect atmospheric conditions, or it can ride animals for miles. Born along by the wind, it can traverse countries and climb mountains. No place is out of reach to all spores; there will always be one that risks – and succeeds.

A spore is an opportunist. Some fruiting bodies can release spores from either sexual or asexual reproduction, dependent on atmospheric conditions, food availability, and the proximity of possible mates. This has led to problems for taxonomists, who named some species twice, unaware that they were observing the same organism's ability to reproduce in different ways. Fungi, it seems, like to hedge their bets: why rely on one method of reproduction, when the other might get better results?

A spore is a health hazard. Many contain allergens that can cause symptoms such as headaches, runny noses, sneezing, earache, coughing, sinus problems and asthma. If you're allergic to fungal spores, you may find yourself struggling throughout much of the year; just as one fungus ends its release of spores, so another begins. There's no escape – even staying indoors might not help you. The spores from moulds, growing quietly on walls, in carpets, on food, in so many different places that you haven't even thought of, can all cause problems for those susceptible.

A spore is a signature. Take a mature mushroom, the flatter the better, and remove the stem. Place the cap, the spore side facing downwards, on a piece of paper. Then cover it with a glass. Leave it for a few hours, maybe longer. When you lift the glass and the cap you'll see a delicate circular design: a spore print. Spray it with hairspray or a fixative, if you want to keep it intact. Spore prints can come in a huge variety of colours, with such fine detail. It is possible to identify a fungus from its spore print: for instance, the Wood Blewit, *Lepista nuda*, creates a pale-pink print so pretty that it seems a shame to eat it – except that the mushroom tastes as good as it looks.

A spore is a soldier, part of a vast army trying to cover the world. There are different legions: the spores of mould, of yeast, of mushrooms, of hidden fungi we can't even see. Viewed through a microscope a spore is no more than a blob, belonging to a form of life with which we cannot hope to empathise, but will continue to anthropomorphise. A spore does not strive, or try, or persevere. It's only a spore.

But we can't help but to be intrigued, and inquisitive. We are, after all, only human.

11

Slow Dancers, Thrown High

It's explosive, a release of intense power with an acceleration speed faster than a bullet leaving a shotgun: the spores of *Pilobolus crystallinus* are jettisoned at a speed of thirty-two kilometres per hour, up into the air, to land a few metres away on fresh, tasty grass, freed from the dung heap on which they grew. They're now in the path of grazing animals once more, so their life cycle can begin again: from mouth to stomach to digestive tract, out of the body, feasting on the nutrients contained within the animal's faeces to create the spores that will fly far and wide once more.

Pilobolus, also known as the Hat Thrower, looks like an unimpressive yellow-white fuzz, squatting on cowpats or sheep dung. If you spy it when you are out walking, you probably won't feel the urge to get too close to it. But it's only in close-up that the delicate structure is revealed. When viewed separately the sporangia (the baglike vessels that contain the spores) are sculptures in glass, tiny transparent tadpoles standing on their tails, their heads trained upwards to the sun as they wait for their moment of escape to come. The pouch of water under each sporangium eventually reaches a pressure that cannot be contained. You won't see the moment of its bursting with the naked eye, but a camera can catch it.

In slow motion *Pilobolus* is weirdly graceful, dancing to its own tune, which we can't hope to hear. The sporangia sway and swell, their heads turning from yellow to black, and then the moment of discharge comes – the acceleration, equivalent to 20,000G, is like watching a rocket launch, straight and strong, while the fungus retracts: buffeted, spent. To put this into perspective, a bullet is fired from a shotgun at an acceleration of roughly 9,000G; this spore release is one of the most powerful forces in nature. It's such an extreme reaction that mycologically minded photographers love to capture it. You can find it online, filmed hundreds of times to be enjoyed as an example of the violent and surprising side of fungi. Some of these films are even set to music, the crescendo timed perfectly with the blast-off of the sporangium on which the camera is tightly focused.

This is not a show of power. *Pilobolus* has developed its explosive technique for good reason: herbivores won't graze too close to their own faeces, so the spores must escape the proximity of their mother fungus for the reproduction cycle to be completed. The farther they are thrown, the better their chances of attaching themselves to vegetation that will be eaten. From grass to mouth via one more trick – the sporangia have a sticky ring of mucus that glues them fast to the stalks on which they land. They won't be shaken off as they are lifted high with the vegetation to become a mouthful.

It's not the determination to reproduce that is unexpected. That's only what we should expect from fungus, and from all life, vying for survival and yet fitting together when and where it suits, to find ways to begin again, and again. It's only that it's a wonder to be human in this time of revelation, capable of understanding such things, and seeing it with our own eyes through the lens of the camera: the slow dancers thrown high, so fast, so strong, finding ways to thrive.

SPREAD

1
Nosing

There's a certain smell I associate with mushrooms. It makes me want to use words like 'rich' and 'earthy'. What a boring set of descriptions, suited to the standard human nose.

I once lived near a large mushroom farm, and sometimes that particular smell would float across the field that separated us and sit over my house, waiting for a door or a window to open so it could come in unannounced and stay for a while, poking around the furniture. *Mushrooms again*, I'd say to myself. *No wonder the house was cheap.*

But I suspect that particular smell, strong and sticky in the nostrils, had less to do with the mushrooms than with the compost and manure they were grown in. The fruiting bodies themselves might have a range of smells that I've simply failed to appreciate. A flick through my identification guides reveals a host of descriptions that have passed me by: mushrooms that smell of shrimp, of sawdust, of radish, plums or parsley, of iodine, of rhubarb, of ammonia or crabmeat. They can smell unpleasant, sickly sweet, rank or rancid. I'm not known for my sense of smell and this is making me wish for a better one. There's an aromatic treasure hunt out there that I'm missing out on, and the prize is the story of a fabled orgasm-inducing mushroom. That must be worth a good sniff. Here goes.

In 2001 two scientists published a report of a smell test they had conducted on thirty-six volunteers. The volunteers smelled an unspecified mushroom of the *Dictyophora* genus that was claimed to be incredibly rare, growing only on the lava floes of Hawaii. Six of the women taking part in the study reported experiencing a mild orgasm at the point of inhaling the smell; all the men said the mushroom smelled 'fetid'.

It's a tiny sample in an unrepeated experiment, but just the thought of it was enough to intrigue many. News outlets all over the world picked up the story and ran away with it. We don't imagine that the sight of an object, any object, would be enough to induce such ecstasy, but the sense of smell is different. It cuddles up to our memories, performing the mysterious task of making us experience certain emotions. Nothing is as evocative as a scent thought forgotten. That might explain why we believe it's possible to take the ultimate pleasure from one.

If some fungi smells are so intense to us, we can only wonder at how incredibly exciting they must be to animals with noses better than our own. A truffle, for instance – truffles have a scent so strong that it can give us headaches, and impregnate every corner of a kitchen so that everything tastes of it. The White Truffle, *Tuber magnatum*, is the most prized in the world for its rich, unique taste. It has long been foraged throughout Italy and Bosnia and Herzegovina, found buried underground, in the shadows of old trees, often oaks. Pigs were traditionally used to root them out, with an enthusiasm that could lead to the truffle being eaten before it could be retrieved for human consumption, so often dogs are trained to do the task nowadays.

The training of the best truffle hounds starts in puppyhood. There are different methods of reward and encouragement, but an initially expensive tactic outlined in the 1925 book *The Romance of the Fungus World*, by F. W. and R. T. Rolfe, sounds a great way to get a dog keen to go to work every morning. From early on in the puppy's life, the Rolfes recommended mixing finely chopped truffle into its usual food, and then, once it has developed a taste for them, burying the truffles nearby and rewarding the puppy once it seeks them out. Then it's only a matter of encouraging the puppy to give up the truffles in exchange for a piece of meat or a chunk of cheese. That sounds easy, but I have to wonder how straightforward that final step in the training regime might be. It would have to be a magnificent cheese to get my attention once I'd been indoctrinated with truffle love from an early age.

Pigs and dogs aren't the only animals that love the smell of truffles. Rodents and insects too flock to the scent, and the Rolfes also mention the use of the truffle fly in the hunt for the good stuff. The larvae live in the truffle itself, so the tiny flies are said to hover there above the ground, usually in the evening, in clouds that can be spotted by those with keen eyesight. Is this one of those methods that has been lost? I can't find any modern mention of it, and there are certainly more reliable methods of finding your truffles, but I love the idea of standing in the forest at sunset, in a glade of oak trees, bent double to look along the ground in the hope of spotting a cloud of flies to give away the position of a rare find.

Some fungi need no such extremes to be found. The stinkhorns live up to their name, and can be seen, and smelled, across the world. *Phallus impudicus*, the Common Stinkhorn, is tall, sturdy and pink-white, developing a slimy bell-shaped head in a darker colour, and a smell of decaying meat so strong that you can smell it from quite a distance. That's the point: it's in the market for attracting as many flies as possible so that the spore-filled slime will stick to their legs and be carried away. The genus name, *Phallus*, was chosen by Linnaeus himself: shaped like an erect penis, it really is hard to miss. Once found, either by sight or smell, never forgotten.

Rich, earthy smells, begone. Instead I'll hunt out the extreme and the tantalising, the disgusting and the delightful. Sawdust and parsley, rancid and mealy, and all the scents of the fungi spread all over the world. Breathe deeply; we're going in.

2

Spire

The woods were cool, damp from an autumn down-pour the night before. I'd walked for hours, lost in thoughts about life elsewhere: my family, back in Devon; the way I didn't seem to fit into student life and my new hall of residence; and the club I'd visited the night before, the music loud enough for my ears to hear it still as a high, thin tone in the silence.

I'd forgotten who I was in that club. The music had taken me over, and the beer had eased that slippery passage into not caring about anything but the moment and myself. My legs were still sore from dancing, and my throat tight from singing along to the lyrics that had suddenly been written only for me. The memory of it made the woods feel soft, enclosed around me like a long dream.

But it's impossible to walk through the woods for long in a trance. There's always some small detail to catch your attention and pull you back, and that day it came in the form of small yellow mushroom growing on a fallen tree.

It was a large tree, roots upended, and it wasn't newly fallen. It looked as if it had been there for months, maybe years – long enough for the fungus to find it and start breaking down its nutrients. The mushroom was a small spot of intense colour: a highlight in a vivid painting of deceptive calm.

It reminded me of home. I looked closely at its bright domed cap, darker at its centre, and the greenish tinge to its gills. I had a feeling I'd seen it often on the moor, during childhood hikes, but hadn't really paid attention to it then. It wasn't rare, or special. Just another mushroom: the centre of its own universe.

I walked around the trunk and was shocked into stillness by the vast yellow carpet that grew on the other side.

The Sulphur Tuft, *Hypholoma fasciculare*, is one of the most common fungi in the UK. It is well known to foragers; it turns up regularly and in large numbers, erupting in clusters, colonising fallen trees with enthusiasm – if only they could be eaten! But no, they're poisonous. A harvest not for humans. I found so many of them, all at once, on that day, feasting on the tree. They were overwhelming, not because of the way they dominated the trunk, but because of what they represented.

Underneath was a mycelial network so large, so strong, that it could create a host of fruiting bodies and send them up to the surface en masse. There would be too many hyphae to count, threads of life finding each other, combining, the minuscule creating the massive.

Sometimes we become aware that we are standing in a presence that dwarfs us.

I've had that feeling a few times in my life: looking up at the sky on a clear night, or through a microscope at the motion of microbes. Entering a cathedral and thinking of the cost of its construction in time and sweat and dedication. There's a sense of wonder to be found in the immense scale of those experiences, and there is also fear. We are insignificant as individuals, even as a species.

If we were to disappear tomorrow, we would not be missed for long, if at all. The cathedrals might stand for a while, as stones do. The microbes will remain in motion and the light of the stars will still shine.

I had the feeling, that day, of standing at the gaudy tip of an enormous creation, and if the tree had turned transparent I would have seen it beneath me, in all its glorious detail of twisted pathways. A body of life, too vast to take in.

I didn't go further. Feeling very small, and more than a little scared, I turned and tiptoed away, the remains of the music still ringing in my ears, and the mushrooms, stuck fast to the top of their spire, unbothered by my presence.

3

The Giant

The poem was called *Whale Nation*. It was written by Heathcote Williams in 1988, and I first heard it in my school's sports hall, when it was delivered by a spoken-word performer who was touring schools in the UK. He delivered that wise, kind collection of reasons to save whales, wrapped up in mesmerising language, with a commitment that I remember well. He angled his head and arms, streamlining his body with slow grace against a background of blue, interspersed with black-and-white images of human cruelty, catching and flensing, turning creatures into oil and perfume. He spoke from memory without pause. It's a beautiful poem.

Blue whales are the largest animals that have ever lived. They can be up to 30 metres long, and they can weigh up to 200 tonnes, which is as heavy as 3,333 humans. They eat only tiny crustaceans called krill, and they can get millions of those in a day. They travel through all the oceans of the world, and cover thousands of miles in a year.

They might be the largest animals that have ever lived, but they are not the largest organisms.

The biggest living specimen of *Armillaria ostoyae* can be found in the Malheur National Forest, Oregon, US. Its mycelial network is estimated to stretch underground for 965 hectares, which is 9,650,000 square metres. You could fit, very roughly indeed, 110,000 blue whales within it. DNA testing has revealed that it's the largest single organism on the planet.

Whales may lend themselves to poetic statements, but I suspect it's harder to write good poetry about fungi. They're difficult to love at times, particularly a genus such as *Armillaria*, which is described in many horticultural and cultivation books as a nightmare for those who want to protect their gardens. It's an indiscriminate killer and can be found happily murdering plants and trees all over the planet. The first you might know of it is when you find its fruiting bodies at the base of a tree in your garden. The mushrooms are – well, they're nondescript, like a million other mushrooms you already think you know, although they do have that gorgeous honey colour to their flat caps. Yellow-white gills turn darker with age, and the stems are quite long and pale. You could eat it, and maybe not find the taste unpleasant, but it can cause an upset stomach. But humanity is not the life form in danger from this fungus.

If the fruiting bodies are breaking out at the base of your tree, then the chances are the fungus has already infiltrated it. It will have slipped its slender black fingers under the bark to create a delicate latticework of rhizo-morphs – thousands of hyphae coming together to create long bootlace-like strands – that can also push directly through soil or travel along existing tree roots to find new victims.

'*Armillaria*' and 'rhizomorph' don't rhyme with much, I suppose, which might be part of the problem when it comes to writing inspirational poetry about them. 'Fungus' rhymes with 'humongous', which gives the *Armillaria ostoyae* its nickname. But I do think this is a subject worthy of dark poetry, for this is a vampire at work, and there's little to beat that for gothic fascination. Above ground, the trees wither and die as it slides along, taking the nutrients it craves voraciously. It's also notoriously hard to kill, like all the best vampires. There's currently no effective weapon against it, although many approaches have been tried to curb its growth, from attempting to rake it painstakingly out of the ground, or plant other trees to see if any can withstand it. So far, no success – and it causes a huge volume of lost timber every year.

What's more – it glows eerily in the dark, having a bioluminescent quality for no discernible reason. Imagine standing alone, in the dark, in the thickest part of night, wrapped in intense, bone-deep cold, knowing that it's underneath you, all around you, for miles, snaking its bootlaces through the soil and up inside the bark of the weak, dying trees that surround you. *It's only a fungus*, you think. *It can't hurt me. There's nothing to be afraid of.*

But you find yourself looking down at the ground, just the same. Looking for the mushrooms, as a sign that it is there. You find them, at the base of a nearby tree: such unimpressive little fruiting bodies. You begin to feel a little better. It might be huge, the Humongous Fungus, but it's not dangerous – at least, to humans. It's not even aware of you, and you can't really see it, beyond these small signs.

Then you see it.

A piece of bark, fallen from the suffering tree to lie beside the mushrooms.

It's glowing.

It has a faint green luminescence. And now your eyes are attuned to it, you begin to see it everywhere, all over the forest. The *Armillaria ostoyae* is a monster, with its fingers in every tree, under every inch of soil. It will grow and grow, and suck away the life of the forest until there is nothing left.

Maybe it doesn't need poetry written about it, but a horror story.

I'll admit that's an overreaction. It's a magnificent organism, worthy of our awe, not our fear. In fact, the more I think about it, the more it seems to me that the Oregon honey fungus and the blue whale have a lot in common. They are the giants of their environments, the sea and the soil, and they must eat vast amounts to maintain their bulk, because that is how the world works. And they are both survivors.

At the time when *Whale Nation* was written, the blue whale population was just beginning to bounce back from the point of extinction. An international ban, not observed by every country, has increased its numbers, although to only a fraction of the population that could be found in the nineteenth century. Still, they live on, finding protected waters. A blue whale can live for up to ninety years.

How about the Humongous Fungus of Oregon? It could be as much as 8,000 years old and it shows no sign of stopping. It reproduces sexually, the mushrooms releasing their clouds of spores to be carried away on the wind. As long as there are trees and plants for it to feed on, and a lack of human interference in its environment, it will survive.

Imagine standing beside such monsters and seeing them clearly. Of course, we can't: that's why we attempt to imagine it, without the barriers of the deep ocean or the dank earth, the impenetrable places. Poetry and stories might come close, but I suspect they could never capture what it's like to be in the presence of these organisms. But perhaps they just give us enough of an idea to make us more aware that we are not the giants of this world, but the caretakers.

4

Walking the Floor

The peace you feel when you walk the forest floor is a lie.

I'm not certain that matters; all kinds of peace are made from lies, or born of a certain perspective, you might say. The human perspective of a forest starts with trees. Trees: the lungs of the planet, the serene organisms living to a different, slower definition of time. What else? Birds. Birdsong, clear above the shush of the leaves. And maybe some small, rustling creatures, keeping out of your way. Squirrels looking down and rabbits peeking out from the places beyond your sight. You can breathe deeply, and walk far within this illusion, while the real work of the forest goes on.

Constant acts of negotiation are taking place: how to describe it? It's a family gathering, everyone shouting in good humour (we hope) to be heard. Or it's a trading floor, negotiating give and take on a grand scale. Or it's a war, with the great trees acting as generals, marshalling the troops below, because everything happens below, under the ground you're walking on. Your perspective is a lofty one.

Fungal hyphae are the very strands of communication living under your feet, forming mycorrhizal associations, making and breaking relationships with the trees. On a very small scale, it might work like this: a tree delivers carbohydrate molecules such as sugars, created through photosynthesis, to the fungus via its roots. In return the fungus spreads further and wider than the roots could ever hope to achieve, at a vastly increased pace, and it finds water, and patches of nutrients to give to the tree in return, or it filters out heavy metals from the soil for the tree's benefit. Imagine that relationship scaled up to include the entire forest, bearing in mind that even a handful of soil will contain thousands of organisms involved in this process – fungi, bacteria, plants, microscopic life forms. Suddenly this forest has become seething, deafening.

Should we call it a kind of city, then? Many have decided that it best resembles that most modern of inventions: the internet. Instead of the worldwide web, we have what's come to be known as the woodwide web, and it's the flow of instant information and resources that makes this an exciting comparison.

I'm not certain any of these descriptions – the trading floor, the family gathering, or even the woodwide web – accurately explains what's happening within a forest. Individual parts that come together to communicate, no matter how efficiently, are still separate units working as one, aligning their own thought processes to a common goal. But a forest does not think. It might make more sense to compare it to the autonomic actions of our own bodies.

For instance, you could explain the act of taking a walk in the forest by saying: *My eyes wanted to see the trees, so they instructed my heart to send extra blood flow to my legs which traded energy, in the form of movement, in return.* It's another perspective, but an odd one; we know bodies don't dissect themselves into cause and effect. Everything works as one. A forest with a strong mycelial network is the same, even to the point of having its own defensive mechanisms. A human body produces pain signals to warn of trouble, and a plant uses the mycelial network to alert others in its vicinity to attacks by insects, such as an aphid infestation, passing on news of its predicament via the underground connections.

If a forest is one organism, then the act of continually chopping down and then replanting trees without consideration of how they are connected makes no sense. As environmentalists and mycologists uncover more information about the mycelial network, it becomes clear that there are ways to work with it that can enable plant growth and health to be improved. Using symbiotic fungi can increase resistance to disease and harsh soil conditions, aid the capture of nutrients, and can even improve crop yields in farming. Further investigation is continuing into whether it could even help clean up pollution. There's still a long way to go when it comes to making sense of this most incredible of underground structures, but the process has begun. And it can't be compared easily to anything within human experience.

That's good. New words will have to be found.

5

Old Stones

Driving down the A303, on the way to Devon, to see my parents, and walk the familiar roads with them. The coastal paths and the dense woods. There are fewer mushrooms now, but then there's less of everything in a world of more.

The traffic slows on the rise that leads up to Stonehenge, every time. People take their time and glance to the right; the view feels like a gift, because we've all become used to paying for such sights. Even at this distance it's obvious that the stones have stood for the longest time. The word that comes to mind is 'weathered'. They look as if the elements have tried to wear them down, but all the rain, snow, sun and ice have managed only to scar the surface, leaving marks and dents, grizzled slopes, and in those scars, lichen live. It's the lichen, more than anything, that give away the age of the monument.

Lichen are not only made of fungi. They are mutualisms. Algae or cyanobacteria live within a structure of hyphae, providing an element of photosynthesis that feeds the fungus, even as the fungus provides them with minerals and a safe home. They grow slowly, surely, and can last for thousands of years on rock faces, but also on trees, or on human structures, among human pollution. Overlooked by many, commonplace and barely noticed, they can be beautiful and strange up close, blooming in patterns that reveal their age and their type.

The lichen of Stonehenge have been surveyed a few times, dating back to 1973 when English Heritage first asked the British Lichen Society (founded by a group of curious investigators in 1958, and home to many passionate and dedicated amateurs on the subject since) to get involved. The number of species found there, growing on the stones, has therefore been catalogued over a period of forty years; some have died out, some have remained, and others have been identified for the first time, leading to hugely interesting discoveries that throw light on the building of that ancient structure. For instance, on the trilithons (two vertical stones with a horizontal stone on top) at least nine types of lichen associated with a maritime environment have been found, leading to the theory that the stones must have been transported to Wiltshire from a coastal area. It's also possible that salt spray from the coast might, in stormy conditions, make it all the way to Salisbury Plain, creating conducive conditions for maritime lichens such as *Ramalina siliquosa* and *Rinodina confragosa* to grow.

A 2013 study of Stonehenge recorded 108 species on the stones. I wonder how many will remain in a hundred years' time, or longer? Whether the road will still run alongside the site, and the weathered stones still bear the telltale blooms of lichen? Maybe, then, we shall properly understand what tales they tell. Now, more than ever, the idea of the importance of mutualisms, of collective organisms, strikes me. We're a long stream of travellers on the A303, all involved in our own individualisms as we reach our own private destinations, but the pressure of collective life we create on an environment is undeniable. The Highways Agency conducted a three-year study of the lichens of Stonehenge, and found species numbers grow and wane. The role of the road on this is, as yet, unclear.

But there's hope to be found in the ability of lichens to endure. They'll survive this road, and what comes after, even as our opinions about them, and about the world, change.

John Wyndham, that great writer of the twentieth century who created triffids, wrote a novel called *Trouble with Lichen* in 1960. A scientist uncovers a species of lichen that holds the key to human longevity – a vastly increased lifespan. Many aspects of the book are interesting but of their time, including the idea that circulating the substance to rich women through beauty products will prevent a global stampede of power-hungry men who want the benefits for themselves. But the question remains: if such a lichen was discovered, how could we ensure it was used fairly? Perhaps the most contemporary opinion one can hold about it is to find it hugely unbelievable that any attempt to use it fairly would be made at all.

It doesn't matter. What does matter is continuing to do what we do best: engaging with the changing world. Human curiosity endures, and it is everywhere, much like lichen. We'll keep looking out of our windows as we travel on, and seeing different things, fresh things, in the view each time, even though they've already been there for centuries, or longer.

6

Under Alice

The largest mushroom in New York City is made of bronze.

It is part of an eleven-foot-tall sculpture that takes you to Wonderland via Central Park. Alice, Lewis Carroll's curious girl, sits on top of an impressive fruiting body with a wide, flat cap that has been polished shiny by climbing children since its construction in 1959.

Alice is not alone. Standing beside her are the White Rabbit, the Mad Hatter, the Cheshire Cat, and other familiar characters from *Alice's Adventures in Wonderland*.

There are also a few smaller mushrooms gathered around to create a shaded space between their thick stalks where the children can crawl and hide: a dark little space, under the protection of those bronze caps. This is a warm and inviting sculpture. It asks you to play, to touch it. It brings an element of fun to the centre of one of the busiest and best-known cities on Earth.

It was created by Spanish sculptor José de Creeft, based on the drawings in the original first edition of the book by English illustrator John Tenniel, and it was cast at the Modern Art Foundry of Long Island City, Queens. It's a product of both New York and the world, which is fitting; no city stands alone. This sculpture is part of a vast, endlessly busy network trading in people, in money, in metal. We're covering the planet in cities that grow ever larger.

NYC is the eleventh largest city in the world, with over 18 million inhabitants, according to the 2018 UN population estimates. The largest, Tokyo, has over twice that number.

Meanwhile, the real mycelial network diminishes, dwindles and is lost.

That's not a surprising statement, considering how routinely we accept loss of diversity nowadays. If the elephants and pandas and rainforests and insects and coral reefs are all disappearing, why shouldn't the same thing be happening under the ground, as we dig down and build up over more and more land? And it's even more difficult to care for the things down there, that we rarely see. Besides, many people dislike mushrooms. There's even a fear of them: mycophobia, born of their sliminess, or their poisonous nature, or of the damp, dark places they're associated with. It would be easy not to care that fungal populations have been in severe decline for decades, or that only 3 per cent of review papers published in mainstream conservation journals discuss that loss, according to the Royal Botanic Gardens Kew *State of the World's Fungi* report of 2018. As fast as we uncover the role of mycelium in our ecosystems we destroy it, and because we did not realise its importance, there's no way of knowing how much has been already lost.

Still, there are mushrooms in Central Park, NYC, and there are those who know where to find them. Regular surveys since 2006 continue to identify hundreds of species in the park, from boletes to puffballs, from corals to lichens. These have all moved into a manmade space – 843 acres of land bulldozed and redesigned in the 1850s to suit a human purpose – and found ways to live around us. Right under our many feet.

And there are also the giant bronze mushrooms, and the children climb them. That can be taken as a symbol of hope, I think. We have a unique relationship with fungi, and it is built on delight as much as on disgust or fear. It's something solid we can climb on, even if the networks running under us right now are mainly of metal and not of mycelium. But we can climb on them, and find a way to make mushrooms of many kinds both commonplace and wondrous again.

7

Expansions

Ladybird. Betty. The Monster. Harold. Zeus. Clint Yeastwood. Brigid. Bubbles. Toxic Ooze. Brett.

The sourdough starter must be the only example of a fungus that gets treated like a pet.

Keen bakers, amateur and professional, name their starters, and feed them up to three times a day. A starter has to be actively managed: divided and used and kept alive so that it can provide the leavening agent – yeast – for loaf after loaf. They can live for decades, and they can be missed when they're gone, each one bringing their own special taste to freshly baked bread.

Although the idea of the sourdough starter has been having a recent resurgence, it is far from new. It predates industrial baker's yeast by thousands of years. The word 'leavened' (meaning 'causes to rise') can be found in the Bible, and describes the process of making fresh dough by using a small part of the mix from a previous batch as the raising agent. But the beginnings of this relationship go back further still. As soon as humans started keeping yeasts, they noticed that some produced tastier bread and beer than others, and so they began to select strains for creating a better result. This form of artificial selection has been judged by modern genetic profiling techniques to date back at least 10,000 years.

A sourdough starter is a strange-looking organism. You mix together flour and water, and let it sit for a few days so that the wild yeast that's in the flour starts to multiply, and there you have it – an off-white blob. Once you get to know its activities, you'll appreciate that it's also a bubbling, thriving mess of fungus squeezed into a jar, busily eating and rising and fermenting in the warm, dark spot where it's being kept. Occasionally it forms a liquid called hooch on its surface. Hooch smells terrible and lets you know that you need to feed your starter. Get rid of some of it, add in some flour and water, and it'll be fine again.

Then, when you want fresh bread, you make your dough as usual and add a piece of your carefully culti-vated starter to it. Knead it in, and you'll have a loaf of tasty sourdough bread to bake in the oven, filled with a fungus you've grown.

Keep feeding and caring for your starter, using a piece of it rather than dried yeast whenever you make bread. Give it a name, if you start feeling fond of it.

All the names I listed at the start of this chapter are those of real sourdough starters as shared by keen home bakers on discussion forums, but the proper sci-entific name for the yeast in your starter is probably *Saccharomyces cerevisiae*. Put it under a microscope, and you'll see it's a collection of rounded cells that can grow incredibly quickly, doubling in number every 100 minutes when the conditions are right. But it can also survive in difficult conditions. It's possible to dry the starter until it is hard and brittle; when lukewarm water and flour is added once more, it'll return to its spongy self.

Hard to kill, and also easy to make: some unbleached flour, a little water, and a few days later, I'll have my own pet starter. What shall I call it? I've been thinking about it, and since Clint Yeastwood is taken, I've decided to opt for Bobby, after US tennis champion Bobby Riggs, who once famously claimed to always rise to the occasion.

That's surely a quality to be admired in both humans and sourdough starters.

8

Once Upon a Beetle

From a certain angle, high above the action, it could resemble a fairy story.

We might say: there's a little busy beetle who lives in a tree in a forest, and tends a fungal garden within. The beetle uses a tiny basket to go out searching for the spores of the fungus it loves, collecting them up and bringing them back to the tree.

I've always loved a good story, and often a tale contains more truth than we might think.

This much is true: the ambrosia beetle eats only cells from the mycelium of ambrosia fungi, so it collects spores of that fungi and takes them to a tree to cultivate them, thereby ensuring its own food source. This is a symbiotic relationship between insect and fungus as the fungus grows in its new home, feeding on the tree, and the beetle then feeds on the fungus. Both the fungus and the beetle win in this relationship. The fungus weakens the tree further, growing quickly, as the larvae of the beetle reach maturity. At that point, the new beetles stock up on spores and set off to find new trees in which to bore their holes, and so the process begins again.

The one part that sounds straight out of a fairy tale is the little basket in which the busy beetle can carry its spores. But that's true too: the ambrosia beetle has a structure on its exoskeleton specifically for carrying fungal spores. Uniting the Latin words for 'fungus' and 'vessel', these containers are known as mycangia – and ambrosia beetles are far from the only insects to have them. Woodwasps, weevils, bark and stag beetles; many insects have a symbiotic relationship with fungi, and come with their own baskets for carrying the spores. In the case of the ambrosia beetle, we're talking about a basket that's a few tenths of a millimetre in size, but it does its job admirably.

If this fairy story was to go on, it might introduce a villain. After all, every story needs one. In this case, it's the lazy beetle that lives, secretly, in the same tree as the busy beetle. The lazy beetle has drilled its own tunnels to reach that fungal garden and is stealing the food for itself.

Again, we're not far from the truth. There is a species of ambrosia beetle that has evolved to feed only on the cells of mycelium cultivated by other beetles. A 2010 study coined a phrase for these thieves: mycocleptic beetles, from *myco* ('fungal') and *cleptic* ('given to stealing'). The process has been going on so long and so successfully that the bodies of those 'lazy' beetles have altered to better suit their needs, with some losing their mycangia over the generations as they have no need to carry spores any more.

You could call this a happy ending for everyone involved – except, of course, for the tree. For some trees, it's a tragedy that is taking place all over the world.

For instance, the Redbay ambrosia beetle made its way to the US in packing-crate material, travelling from South East Asia, and has since been devastating plant species across the eastern states. It's not so much the beetles causing the damage with their tunnelling, but the fungus they're carrying: *Raffaellea lauricola* causes the disease Laurel Wilt, weakening and killing members of the laurel family, including trees such as the redbay. Thousands across South Carolina and Georgia have been destroyed. Evidence of Laurel Wilt has also been found in crops, such as the avocados farmed in Florida. Attempts to control the spread of Laurel Wilt include tactics such as 'quarantining' affected trees – keeping or destroying them at their original sites so that the beetles don't spread.

Or how about the southern pine beetle? It's an insect native to the south-eastern US, but expanding its reach, working its way up the coast to New York State and beyond. The beetle's tunnels are damaging enough, but it carries Blue Stain Fungi, of the *Ascomycota* species – between them they have led to the loss of billions of dollars for the timber industry.

Perhaps the most famous example, Dutch Elm Disease, has infected a vast number of elms globally. It is spread by bark beetles who carry microfungi of the same species, *Ascomycota*, in their mycangia. The elms attempt to plug up the tunnels bored by the beetles to protect themselves, but the process also stops water and nutrients from being able to travel up the trunk. The trees end up starving themselves to death.

This is definitely not a fairy tale. It's still a great story, though, of luck, and environment, and change. If we told it from the point of view of the fungus, we might say:

Once upon a time there was a fungus.

The fungus grew well in areas where rotting wood, its food supply, was most plentiful. And it grew best when its spores just happened to get carried into the rotting wood by the busy beetles that were always scurrying around it.

The process of growing well and growing best continued for millions of years, and the fungus and the beetle both benefited and changed from their association. The beetles that survived a little longer from some small genetic benefit, such as a depression in their exoskeleton in which spores of the fungus collected, passed on their benefits to more of the next generation, and so on, and so on, and so on, so that a partnership became a symbiotic relationship so successful that it conquered the world, and both the beetles and the fungi lived. Maybe not happily, and maybe not forever, but they did live, which is better than millions of species that came before, and will come after, them.

This is a tale of evolution.

9
Seven Ways to Survive

Idreamed of travelling. In my school textbook there were seven continents, and in my mind there were great wonders on them that I was desperate to see. I made a list of manmade and natural things, without really thinking of the differences between them: the Eiffel Tower, Angel Falls, the Grand Canyon, Abu Simbel. They all existed separately, drawn on an imagined canvas.

I remember learning about the continents in terms of tectonic plates and land mass, but never really connecting them to the creatures that lived on them. They were empty spaces, and biology was a separate subject on a different day. But the more I read and see, the more I find myself trying to piece together the puzzle of the world. How do we all live on it? How do we fit? So, let's take a brief tour of this world, and see how fungi thrive and survive within it. Let's fill this blank canvas with the strange, wonderful forms of life that often get overlooked for prettier sights.

You could start in the European forests that remain, under the dense, dark canopy of beech trees that began to dominate the landscape after the Ice Age. Beech grows thick, crowding out other contenders, creating a harsh environment that presents unique challenges, but there is still much beauty and diversity to be found there. If you were to walk through one of the ancient beech forests that have been brought under human protection (a strange concept, but a necessary one – you can find them throughout Continental Europe, from Ukraine to Spain) you will come across *Oudemansiella mucida* – the Porcelain Fungus, also known as the Poached Egg Fungus. Their glistening white caps are attached to thin stems that curve to maintain a permanently horizontal position, and they jut out from rotting beeches in clusters, translucent and slimy as jellyfish. There's an elegant, otherworldly quality to the way they climb high on the trunks, looking down on us mere humans from their vantage points.

You won't find other fungi around them. They have a secret weapon. They produce their own fungicide to keep the beech trees all to themselves. The type of fungicide they make, strobilurins, is so effective that it has since been synthesised for agricultural use, but it originates from wood-rotting fungi such as the *Oudemansiella mucida* and the *Strobilurus tenacellus*; we've stolen their secret for our own benefit, but left the fungus itself alone in these deep, protected forests – thin flesh and mucal texture mean they are far from good to eat, even if they aren't poisonous.

After a walk through the woods, you could move on to Asia, and a trek through the Himalayas. These mountains are spread across Bhutan, India, Nepal, Pakistan and China, their peaks some of the highest in the world, and they are sacred to many who live in their shadows. But the land is not only cold and bare. So many forms of life thrive here, from the subtropical areas in the lower elevations to the permanent snow of the peaks.

The Tibetan plateau is known as 'The Roof of the World'. It is surrounded by mountains and studded with lakes: you can find forests and meadows, tundra and desert. And you can treat yourself to one of the most expensive fungi in the world: *Ophiocordyceps sinensis*, also known as Caterpillar Fungus. It colonises the body of the ghost moth larva in winter, then breaks through its head come the spring to produce a fruiting body. The larva, shrivelled and sucked dry, looks like nothing more than a dry twig when this process is complete. And the fruiting body of the fungi is unimpressive too; there's nothing wondrous to see here, but the thought of the vampiric conquest of a living being to the slow, sucking growth of the fungus inside it is a powerful, queasy one – although not enough to affect the demand for *Ophiocordyceps sinensis* in Chinese medicine. It is highly prized, the larvae and the fruiting bodies ground into a powder to be used as an aphrodisiac. Over a million people living on the Tibetan plateau sell the fungus to make a living.

But climate change and over-harvesting are having an impact on this business. The fungus has colonised the larvae, and now we take over the fungus. There's no place or method to escape us.

Onwards, then, to Australasia, but not necessarily deep into the outback. Instead, stick more closely to the gardens and leaf piles of houses to find, nestling in the grass, a fungus that can't be missed. It's red, sometimes scarlet, and so vivid that you might think it's in the wrong environment, and you should be standing on the seashore: the Anemone Stinkhorn, properly known as *Aseroe rubra*.

Whatever you call the many reaching appendages it has – tendrils or tentacles, arms or legs – the way they snake free to stand proud from its egglike centre is eye-catching. They stretch out, asking you to get closer. But if you do come across one, you might want to keep a distance. The top of the fungus lets out a fetid smell, as strong as decomposing meat, wafting from its gleba – a slimy spore-filled substance. Its job is not to keep predators away but to attract those creatures that find such odours irresistible. Flies land in a frenzy, and feed on the sugary gleba, ingesting the spores and then spreading them further afield in their faeces. This is a mutually beneficial relationship: the flies get a good meal and the *Aseroe rubra* gets to reproduce at a scope beyond its reach.

We humans have helped this stinkhorn to be successful beyond its wildest dreams. Since the nineteenth century we have been fascinated by this weird form, and have carried specimens out of the grass, and then across the seas, to cooler climates, where it has also managed to gain a foothold in the wild. Sometimes being big, bold and difficult to ignore can have its uses; you can now find *Aseroe rubra* making its stench and happily attracting its flies in the United Kingdom and the United States.

Speaking of which, the next continental stop is North America, vibrant and impossibly varied, where some forms of life are beginning to reassert themselves after coming close to extinction. Off the west coast of California you'll find the Channel Islands – an archipelago that was once given over to agricultural and military purposes but is now a national park and a marine sanctuary. There are too many rare and recovering species here to count, and one of the most recently named is the lichen *Caloplaca obamae*.

There's no informal name to give; lichen often don't seem to inspire common names, perhaps because they rarely catch our attention. This one lives only on Santa Rosa, on the rock terraces that rise above the Pacific on the north side of the island, and it's also hardly thrilling to gaze on, particularly in a place that holds so much natural beauty. If you can tear your eyes away from the blue-green sea and the soft strip of sandy coast, then you'll see a scattering of orange granules on the raised, crusty surface of the rock. It's a cooperation of fungi and algae, locked in a mutualistic relationship, both benefiting from the arrangement.

If change is our constant, we can see it in the form of *Caloplaca obamae* as it quietly returns to abundance. The cattle that were grazing it to extinction since the 1850s were removed from Santa Rosa and it took its opportunity to grow, out of our sight, out of our minds. Then, in 2007, a lichen curator from the University of California, Riverside, noticed it, wrote about it, and named it after Barack Obama as a token of appreciation for the president's support of science education. A human label for a collection of organisms that work together as one: is this an encouraging fungal story? Maybe we can find inspiration in this recovery and discovery – we don't have to dominate the world at the cost of all others, after all.

Down to South America, for a stop in Venezuela. Not to see Angel Falls, however much my childhood self might have dreamed of it, but to the Guayana region, with its plains and highlands, mangroves and rainforests. It's an overwhelming sensation for the eyes and ears in all its towering growth, and it's the home of the Jotï: an indigenous group that lives in small communities, hunting and gathering what it needs from the rainforest. The Jotï's diet includes mushrooms, but they have their own unique mythology around the fungi they find, categorising some as food meant only for predatory spirits, known as *awëladï*, making them dangerous to handle. Others are thought to be medicinally beneficial. One particular species is known as Spider Monkey Bile Mushroom (*waña yakino*); yellow-green in colour, it is thought to restore the luck and skill of the hunter who eats it.

The Jotï have many stories about mushrooms, their uses, and their symbolism, stretching back to the beginning of the world. Stories are easier to remember, and learn from – knowledge can be passed from generation to generation, helping those who come after to deal with the *awëladï* that surround them. But the dangers they face are so numerous: the ones that are invisible, and the mechanical ones that spring from the modern world, eating up entire rainforests, mushrooms and all.

To continue the journey by sailing eastwards to Africa, what fungi could you find in the hot stretch of the savannah, grassland with little rainfall and sparse, set-apart trees? Maybe start by examining the trunks of the baobabs, those ancient deciduous giants that can store thousands of gallons of water in their hollow trunks. They have long occupied the savannah, and they are dying.

In the last decade it's been estimated that up to 70 per cent of the baobabs of South Africa have perished, and symptoms of their fatal illness have included a powdery black substance on their bark, making a splotchy pattern, resembling rust. Scientists from the University of Pretoria examined affected specimens in 2015 and identified four types of fungi living on the trees, including a new species, which they named *Rachicladosporium africanum*. Together, these fungi were classed as causing 'black-mould syndrome', penetrating the bark of the baobabs and causing a wound reaction. Was the syndrome to blame for their deaths?

Climate change is the most probable reason. Baobabs need so much water to survive, and rain has been in short supply in South Africa for the past decade, and longer still. But fungi such as *Cladosporium* are opportunists, and they'll use the tree's weakness to their advantage, spreading widely, swelling their numbers. Black mould is the symptom, not the cause of this illness. Fungi, just like the rest of the Earth's organisms, have to find a way to live in the world humans are creating, even to the detriment of others.

Finally, to Antarctica, which we think of as pristine, bare of life.

It's hard to imagine that there's a connection to the black mould on the baobabs of Africa, but there are wood-rotting fungi living on this continent too – even though the only wood available is a human relic. Three small huts, built between 1901 and 1911, remain from the attempts of Scott and Shackleton to explore Antarctica, and fungi are feeding on them as they break down.

The black spots found on the wood were studied in 2003 by Robert Blanchette, an expert in the study of how fungi affect archaeological artefacts. He found *Cadophora*, both known and new species, a soft-rot fungi that can exist in extreme conditions all over the world. Often they struggle to compete with other fungi in more temperate environments; in the extreme cold, they had the huts

to themselves. They don't love the cold but can toler-
ate it. As the region continues to warm, they'll become
more active, eventually putting the huts at risk of col-
lapse. But then they'll also find they have competition,
as Antarctica opens up to both natural and manmade
expansions. Maybe, then, the *Cadophora* will soon find
their one advantage taken away.

From the dry pages of my geography textbook I learned
about the continents, and dreamed of visiting them.
They seemed separate to me, but the truth is that everywhere, in all the places I wanted to see, the same types of
organism find ways to grow. There are no blank canvases;
wherever I look, wherever I go, life is already there, waiting for me.

10

Stowaways of the Space Age

Humans are bags of fragile bones and organs that need to be kept in precisely the right conditions to flourish. But we push at the limits of those conditions all the time, daring to see how far we can go: the hottest, the coldest, the lowest, the highest we can bear, using our ingenuity to design ways to survive.

Fungi doesn't need to be so clever. Some fungi can survive in extreme temperatures and without oxygen.

They can lie dormant and wait for the right conditions to wake up, warm up, spread. They can grow in soil, in wood, on plastic, on pollution. Why wouldn't they be able to survive space?

We already know that they can – at least, within the confines of human-built space stations, where many types of fungi have successfully grown, sometimes in a monitored capacity as part of experiments to ascertain the viability of different kinds of life in those conditions, and sometimes . . . not.

Mir, the first modular space station, was built in low orbit around the Earth in 1986 – what a feat of science and engineering – and it operated as a research laboratory until its orbit decayed in 2001. In my mind, when I think of it, I picture *Mir* as a perfect, clean environment, innovative and experimental. But this was not so; those who visited *Mir* commented on first being hit by the smell. British chemist Steve Pearce described it as a mixture of sweaty feet, nail-polish remover, body odour and vodka, among other things. He later attempted to recreate the smell as part of a NASA experiment. This unique scent could be due, in part, to the stowaways on board *Mir* that came as a shock to the astronauts: bacteria and fungi, found living happily behind panels, on spacesuits, on cables and around window frames. The discovery led to a flurry of news articles at the time. If you ever wondered if fearmongering in the media has extended to fungi, then take a look back at the BBC News article of Thursday, 8 March 2001, entitled 'Mutant Fungus from Space'. All it lacks is an exclamation mark or two to turn it into a 1950s science-fiction movie. With *Mir* about to return to Earth, the article moots the idea that the fungi on board will have mutated to the point where they can do 'serious damage to humanity'.

The International Space Station, first launched in 1998, has had similar fungal issues, and study suggests that those fungi with high quantities of melanin thrive in space-station conditions, being better suited to resist high radiation levels. The genera of fungi that have been found surviving in the ruins of the reactor of Chernobyl, such as *Cladosporium*, have also been discovered on board the ISS, along with *Penicillium* and *Aspergillus*. The possibility of mutation, caused by the effect of radiation, remains under investigation, although the real area of concern continues to be fungi that can survive outside craft, exposed to open space, rather than within the human-friendly confines of a space station. An organism that grows over solar panels, say, or gets into the exterior sections of a multi-million-dollar craft, to cause havoc right in those very places that cannot be reached without extreme difficulty, could jeopardise the future of space travel.

This is not purely a theoretical area of concern. There are fungi that, amazingly, survive in open space. A 2009 Russian experiment into space exposure called Biorisk revealed that both *Aspergillus versicolor* and *Penicillium expansum* underwent changes while exposed for seven months that helped them to survive, increasing their layers of melanin to resist radiation.

If a space station makes for happy fungi, and even open space doesn't necessarily present a problem, then where next? NASA has been investigating the possibility of using mycelia to create living shelters on Mars using melanin-rich fungi to absorb radiation and protect the human inhabitants within. If mycelia can create strong, flexible structures on Earth then they might well offer such possibilities elsewhere, and they could be constructed, effectively grown, on location, making them easier to transport. They also offer the proposal of easy, organic disposal after use, putting little strain on the alien environment.

A mycelial home on Mars – a magnificent achievement for both man and fungi, if the success of a species lies in its ability to adapt to the most challenging of conditions. We have both done just that: we erupt from our planet, in our rockets, with our plans. We are both destined to spread. And we will, eventually and inevitably, decay.

DECAY

1

Gathering the Dead

Finding a puffball is a perfect gift.

The giant puffballs, *Calvatia gigantea*, swell large in the field, some smooth and unpatterned, some puckered and speckled. Slice one open, and if you're lucky you'll find it to be white and firm inside. Take it home and fry it, dipped in egg and breadcrumbs – not too much butter – until it turns golden brown. It tastes mildly nutty, although maybe that's just the butter. But I'm sure there's also a hint of earthy flavour to each mouthful that only mushrooms have. It's a connection to the ground.

But before you can admire its white flesh, you need to cut it free of the field.

Take a sharp knife. There are specific knives you can get for foraging, sharp and curved and a good fit in the palm. Slice the puffball through at the stem. Then turn it upside down and examine the base.

Maggots.

The fly will take advantage of the short life of the mushroom, laying eggs within so that its offspring can eat the fruiting body of a fungus as it starts to break down. It makes a great home for many insects, and we tend not to see them even though we're probably eating them in large numbers. Pick what seems to be a perfectly fresh mushroom and then leave it out to dry, and you might well find at least a few starved maggot corpses falling from the gills before long, the flesh of the mushroom toughening to the point of inedibility – for them, at least.

The US Food and Drug Administration stipulates that up to twenty maggots per 100g of drained mushrooms or 15g of dried mushrooms is acceptable for human consumption, so freshly picked or mass produced, you'll be likely to eat a maggot or two at some point if you're a mycophile.

All life ends in death, and all stories have an end.

Flies and fungi are both organisms that thrive on decay, and are a necessary, if not always loved, part of the life cycle. They're a reminder that the world does not revolve around us, and does not end with us. Pick a puffball and slice it open: inside you might find firm, white flesh that is good for us to eat. Or you might find a yellow or brown, pulped mess, and a stalk that's a good home for maggots. Either way, for humans or insects, it's a perfect gift.

2

The Big Stick

Some mushrooms are not quite killers, and this story is not quite true.

The girl is given a big stick. She's young, small for her age, and her hand reaches barely halfway up the knotted wood. The weight of the stick is reassuring.

'Ready?' asks the guide, and they set off into the *Schwarzwald*, the Black Forest, in search of mushrooms.

This first trip overseas is a milestone for her. She is spending a week in a village in the south east of Germany where grape-growing is a major industry, the sun is much hotter at midday than her skin can easily take, and the early-morning pastime at the weekend – at least for her host family – is hunting or foraging in the black woods on their doorstep. They are well prepared and she has been kitted out properly for the task, and reminded of the essential rule, which is the same in any language: don't touch. So she is ready to plunge into the forest and find some extraordinary sights. Perhaps even as extraordinary as the father and the guide of this family: a short, stocky man with meaty hands, sharp blue eyes and an impressively bushy moustache. She is afraid of him and a little in awe: here is a man who could survive using only those hands and his knowledge. She walked in the woods every day at home, but she's just beginning to appreciate that she doesn't really understand them, not in the way this man does.

But in truth, once she starts walking, she can see it isn't that different from her experiences at home: the darkness cast by the canopy, the crunching of leaves underfoot. She relaxes a little. She has been told that she might see a fox, a badger, or even a wild boar, which makes her clutch that stick like a weapon at times, but there is no sudden snorting, or eruption of a hairy beast into the clearing. It is both a relief and a disappointment. But mushrooms – those she sees.

It helps to go hunting with an experienced forager. The father knows places to look, logs to lift. The damp and productive parts of the forest. He points out some species, then cuts others cleanly at the base of their stems and puts them in the old wooden basket on his arm. He never takes all the mushrooms he finds, leaving some for others, or covering some of the smaller ones over gently with leaves.

Just at the point where she is beginning to notice that the stick is heavy and her feet are tired, he crouches down and points to a slope of grassy earth leading to a big oak tree. 'No,' he says. He looks at her with his bright blue eyes. '*Kaput*. Dead.'

Now this is the level of danger she has signed up for. She approaches cautiously, hoping for something that proclaims its toxicity in strong colours. An oozing scarlet mess with dead animals lying around it. A bright, bold beacon of beware.

What she sees is a fairly small, slightly greenish mushroom.

It looks a lot like all the other mushrooms that the

father has been putting in his basket. How can he be so sure? He sees the doubt in her eyes.

'Dead,' he repeats, and steers her around it.

A brush with death can be an ordinary business.

He is pointing out possibly the most poisonous mushroom on the planet. It is slightly green with a smooth cap, shining among the slippery, piled autumn oak leaves.

It is an *Amanita phalloides*.

The lethal dose is thought to be small. Ingesting half a cap would probably kill an adult, and it has killed many – thirty-eight of the thirty-nine fatal mushroom poisonings in Britain between 1920 and 1950 were caused by it. It contains more than one poisonous compound, and they take their time to kill you. When you first eat an *Amanita phalloides* you'll have a severely upset stomach, vomiting and diarrhoea; then you might think you're getting better. It'll take a few days longer for your liver and kidneys to fail. There's no cure.

The common name for it is the Death Cap.

Emperor Claudius was thought to have been murdered with a dish of mushrooms, possibly *Amanita phalloides*, fed to him by his power-hungry wife, Agrippina, so that her son Nero could become emperor. At least, that was what the Roman populace believed in 54 CE, when the official story that he had been struck down unexpectedly while watching some actors perform didn't convince anyone. It seems that we've known about the danger of the Death Cap for a really long time – but that hasn't made us any better at identifying them.

Shouldn't poisonous mushrooms come with a warning? The sting of a wasp comes wrapped in yellow and black. A poison-dart frog can be a range of intense colours, each one screaming a warning. A foxglove is bright, burning pink, and will kill you if you disobey that clear instruction not to eat. And there are some mushrooms that are happy to use the colour-coded system of danger – the Poison Fire Coral, *Podostroma cornu-damae*, is native to Asia and resembles warped fat fingers, held up from the ground. It's a pinkish-red stop sign: eating it will bring on multiple organ failure. If only all the toxic things displayed themselves with such clarity.

For every showy killer there's a nondescript one. The equivalent of the quiet neighbour you never really knew, going about their business; the taipan, a snake of uniform brown, sliding away from human interference until it is really forced to bite; the brown recluse spider, tiny and keeping to itself in a log pile or a shed until it's disturbed, when it delivers a bite filled with necrotic venom. When it comes to mushrooms the Deadly Webcap (*Cortinarius rubellus*) would be comparable, which you might find in a pine forest in Scotland or northern Europe. It's brown, just like our snake and spider: that boring shade of brown that makes it easy to underestimate. In Peter Marren's 2012 book *Mushrooms* he describes it as 'dangerously bland' which is a perfect summation of its threat. It could easily be mistaken for something edible, missed amid a collection of other fungi, fried up, and placed on a table only to cause kidney failure and possibly death.

Such scary, seemingly innocuous, things remind me of a famous phrase that was coined by Theodore Roosevelt, in a letter he wrote in 1900: 'Speak softly, and carry a big stick.'

Poison is a very large stick. But if you can't manage to be poisonous, you can pretend to be, either by advertising a warning with a colour scheme that you don't really deserve to use, or even looking just like your very dangerous neighbour. That's the case with the False Death Cap, *Amanita citrina*, which could well be mistaken at a distance for the deadly version. But *Amanita citrina* has a pleasant smell, similar to potatoes, whereas the Death Cap smells rotten. It's still not good to eat, but to do so wouldn't kill you horribly.

The girl is lucky, in the forest, that the experienced father knows exactly what he is doing, and what to pick. Mushroom-hunting is always a mission with an element of peril, even though it might not look like it.

He takes the basket of mushrooms home, and tells the girl to leave the big stick at the edge of the forest.

And the girl eats the mushrooms picked for dinner that night, and the next day she goes home, back to her family.

She develops a healthy fear of innocuous-looking things, from snakes to spiders, neighbours to nature. And she starts to write. She writes strange, not quite true, stories about softly spoken organisms with her pen, her very own little stick, clutched tightly between her fingers at all times.

3

Fire, Faith and Gangrene

T he sixteenth-century woodcut shows a tall, bearded
man from which straight lines emerge to create a
burst of radiant light. He has a bright circle behind his
head: a halo. Animals shelter in his long robe, and he
holds an open book and a staff. He is wise and venerable.
He is Anthony the Great, born around 250 CE: a monk
in his lifetime, a saint since his death, and the Father of
All Monks.

There are many representations of him; Hieronymus
Bosch painted a triptych of him in roughly the year 1500.

He has comforted thousands, even millions, through the centuries, being named in their prayers, asked for aid as they attempted to overcome the worst diseases of their times. And, for a long time, ergotism – poisoning due to eating the fungus *Claviceps purpurea* – was commonly known as St Anthony's Fire.

A wonderful story explains this link. Long after St Anthony's death, when his saintly status was already established, his bones were moved to France and kept in a church in the south-eastern region of Dauphiné. The son of the richest nobleman of that region was afflicted with ergotism, and so the nobleman swore, faithfully, on the tomb of St Anthony: 'Save my son, and I will help you to save others.' The son recovered, and the nobleman was true to his word. He used his wealth to create a new order of monks dedicated to caring for the sufferers of ergotism, and the story goes that the first monastery for this purpose, built in 1093, had brightly coloured walls, as red as fire.

Looking at that woodcut again now (found that first time while flicking randomly through the pages of an old book taken down from a high shelf, my attention arrested by the image) it's not the saint I stare at, but the figure at his feet. A man half-crouches before him, his face etched with both awe and pain. The man has raised an arm wreathed in flame. He holds it out in supplication: 'Please, heal me.' He feels he is on fire. It tingled, at first. Then the tingling turned to burning in his limbs, and he could only walk awkwardly, staggering and falling often under his own twisted weight. His stomach is agony, too, and he can't think straight. He suffers from hallucinations and convulsions. He doesn't know it, but his veins are constricting, and his extremities are not getting enough blood flow. Gangrene will set in soon.

All because of the dark bread he ate.

The bread was made from rye, growing well in a wet year, and if the stalks had been examined closely before they were harvested, it would have been possible to see *Claviceps purpurea* in action, taking the place of some kernels with its own growths of curved, purplish black bodies. Fungi of the genus *Claviceps* can grow on many types of cereal, but they are much harder to spot on rye; this time, the farmer and the baker have missed the evidence of contamination, and the fungus has been milled along with the grains, and baked, and eaten.

The figure in the woodcut is probably not alone. If he's eaten ergot-laced bread, the chances are many others of his village have too. But it's easier to represent the suffering of the community, many communities, through that one man, practically kneeling, his expression captured in a state of desperation. Although he is secondary to the glory of the saint, it's the image of that man that stays with me, and makes me thankful that we live in an age of fungicides and modern farming knowledge, even though we now understand that these can create their own problems too.

Epidemics of St Anthony's Fire were devastating for thousands of years, right into the twentieth century, at which point farming techniques such as deep-ploughing and crop rotation became commonplace ways of stopping ergot from germinating. *Claviceps purpurea* has been suggested as the cause behind events that seem inexplicable to us now, from the Salem witch trials to the dancing manias that occurred in medieval Europe. Periods of intense and strange behaviour within towns and villages could possibly be attributed to one particular element of the fungus's effect: its hallucinogenic quality. Science has isolated and seized on this; LSD was first synthesised from ergot in 1938. When God or the devil would once have been held to blame, perhaps the real culprit was living in the fields, swaying on the stalks of rye.

St Anthony remains a powerful figure. His feast day is celebrated in Orthodox and Catholic churches, and he continues to inspire works of art, novels and films. It's never been an uncomplicated relationship – that of the saint to the sufferer. But once, for the terrible illness of ergotism, there was only faith and St Anthony's monks to offer hope against the fire. For me, the figures in the woodcut, with and without haloes, are a reminder to be glad to live in a time where faith alone does not have to be enough, and some fungi can be fought.

4

Where the Rule Bends

'Magic' is a word used to cover many types of manipulation, from the sleight of hand of a trained entertainer to acts so huge that they remake the world. It can bend all the rules of reality, defeating death and rewinding time. At least, in our imaginations.

During my time at university I had a friend who liked to go out roaming the fields, searching for cow dung on which *Psilocybe semilanceata* might be growing. They're also known as Liberty Caps, named after the distinctive shape of the pointed hats worn by French revolutionaries, but the common name for those unassuming little fruiting bodies, and other fungi that contain the compound psilocybin, is a familiar one: Magic Mushrooms.

He never did find any, as far as I'm aware, although I'm not sure he would have told me if he had. I had that innocent, confused look back then that gave away the fact I was better suited to looking at life than taking part in it. I suspect he was like me, on some level, and really wouldn't have known what to do with them if he had come across them. Maybe it would have been enough for him to track them down and stare at their waxy brown bonnets and slender stalks.

My friend was looking for something more than the mushroom. He sought a sense of transgression, of possibility outside our mundane reality, but such things, when found, take courage to grasp by the stem. Or possibly all it takes is a lack of awareness of the UK law that classes the act of picking, producing or possessing any fungus that contains the substance psilocybin as a Class A drugs offence.

Psilocybin is similar in chemical make-up to lysergic acid diethylamide: LSD. It can cause a sensation of intense euphoria in those that consume it, and could lead to hallucinations and synaesthesia; music might take on colour, or words might possess a scent. The rules of reality are bent in ways that might delight or terrify. Can a person backtrack, after such an experience? Can the world ever return to normal?

There are some trips from which we never return.

Death, the final trip, comes with rules too, or possibly the illusion of rules, or of reality itself. It is the place where expectations end, so perhaps it doesn't really matter. We don't know what death means, or what waits beyond it, if anything. But we all have one thing in common: we want it to be painless and fearless, when it comes for us.

Painlessness is the remit of medicine. How to achieve fearlessness? Can the medical world deliver that too? Recent studies of psilocybin have shown its use can help those who might be approaching death to feel less sad or anxious. Trials conducted have shown that patients with life-threatening cancers who received a high dose of psilocybin (versus a low dose, or a placebo) reported an increase in optimism and quality of life, and a decrease in death-related anxiety and depression. A 2016 trial conducted by scientists at Johns Hopkins University School of Medicine, Baltimore, concluded that the effect of a high dose could last as long as six months. Further investigations have taken place into the possibility of psilocybin use helping the bereaved, or suicidal, or those who are struggling to deal with life in a modern world disconnected from nature – researchers at Imperial College London found that the use of psilocybin increases the perception of the user as being part of nature, one planet, at a time when many are suffering from sorrow for the world that is being lost – 'climate grief'.

This isn't magic, in any sense of the word. It's only a possibility that needs further study. But it does make me think that sometimes rules need to be reconsidered, rather than broken or bent. Socrates wrote about death, 'People fear it as if they knew for certain it is the greatest evil.' The rule that says that the process of the end of life should be viewed as terrifying – can it be rewritten? To have a tool created from a small brown mushroom that could help those coming to the end of our reality to accept, to welcome, to find a quiet and peaceful release: that would truly be magical.

5

Killer Club

Alone carpenter ant is the millionth cog in a machine. It completes its tasks, keeping food coming in and waste going out of the part of the forest its nest has claimed. One ant is no more remarkable than any other, even though tasks may vary; there is no individual thought. The nest is a mechanism of survival, well oiled. An insectile industry.

But machines can always malfunction. All it takes, in the case of a lone carpenter ant, is a genus of fungus called *ophiocordyceps*.

A spore from *Ophiocordyceps unilateralis* happens to find its way on to the exoskeleton of a carpenter ant. It gets inside, and a hijacking process begins. It's a single cell that starts to replicate in the bloodstream, and then those cells connect to each other, growing in and between the ant's muscles, creating chains of cells that will make the ant part of an entirely different machine. Cogs are pieces that can fit into so many mechanisms. Now part of a different life cycle, no longer serving the nest, the ant is compelled to obey the fungus instead. And the fungus commands it to climb.

It climbs a plant stem to the height of 25 centimetres – a precise number to ensure a certain amount of heat and humidity for the fungus to grow. Then the ant sinks its mandibles into the base of a leaf, and does not let go, even during the process of the fungus erupting from the top of the ant's head, even after death. The fungus creates a long, questing stalk, reaching up, and then forms a club shape at its tip, filled with spores. The spores are released. They fall down, past the still-gripping mandibles of the ant, past the plant, to the ground around the nest, into the paths taken by the living carpenter ants who are still at work. And the cycle begins again.

This is not about putting an order, a desire that cannot be ignored, within the ant. It's not a form of brainwashing, or zombifying. The brain of the ant remains untouched by the fungus. The muscles, the body, are controlled by *Ophiocordyceps unilateralis*, but not the mind. Who needs the mind, anyway? Direct control is much easier and has proven to be extremely effective; this fungus can wipe out an entire nest of ants, and has been keeping the ant population in check for millions of years. A fossilised leaf from 48 million years ago was found to show the marks of an ant's 'death grip' around a leaf stem, caused by the fungus, creating the earliest record we have of behavioural manipulation in the natural world.

But whenever there is a long-standing predator, there is a defence mechanism, and ants are no different. If ants come across the body of one of their kind, mandibles wrapped tightly around a leaf stem, the ant machine mobilises into action, prompting ants to remove it, to take it as far from the nest as they can manage. Ants, and other social insects at risk from parasitism such as honeybees, have also shown mutual grooming behaviours that might help to remove the threat.

You could say the ant nest and the life cycle of the

Ophiocordyceps unilateralis are locked in advanced warfare, in a battle that has been raging for longer than we've been on the planet. But I prefer not to give it a human angle, or to put it down to brains, or sides. This isn't a zombie war. It's a honed and precise happening, a product of survival, for insects and fungi alike.

What I find most fascinating is that even though there are millions of moving parts in these mechanisms, only one small cog can bring down the entire machine. A lone spore falls on a carpenter ant. A lone ant climbs a stem . . .

6

Underground Visions

Perhaps there is only one fear, and that is death. The question becomes how it might arrive, and so we fear falling, or drowning, or getting bitten or stung; we are scared of the methods of delivery because they give shape to the formless end. I had a friend who told me she was certain she would be stabbed to death one day. She couldn't bear to use a sharp knife because of a dream she'd had. A faceless figure drove a blade in deep, to the stomach, and then a darkness fell on her that stretched on until she finally woke. I asked her if the dream or the darkness was worse, and she said she didn't know.

It's highly unlikely that you'll get killed by a fungus. But do you fear them?

The mycophobic among us may fear the mushroom itself, or they may fear the illnesses that spores and mould can bring, springing from the damp corners of the bathrooms, or floating along in the air, penetrating lungs, lodging within. Black speckles and the smell of mildew: the thought of dying from a wet, dark disease.

And it's not only the thoughts of how a person might die, but the image of what comes next, when the fungus gets to work. It's a vision of the body after death: colonised, utilised, broken down and rebuilt into fat, healthy fungal growth, the slippery eruptions from the sucked-dry corpse. Yes, there are things to fear here. Writers of the weird and horrific have been enjoying writing about them for a long time, and their focus has long been on the act of the fruiting body. It's the change represented by the growth from the ground, a mutation from the mushroom to a man, say, or being caught between such states. We know we will be taken over by fungi one day, but we really don't want to be there to see it happen. Fear and fascination for that final process are fused.

At the turn of the twentieth century, William Hope Hodgson discovered the use of the mycological to inspire horror in his seafaring stories. In *The Voice in the Night* (1907), a lone sailor rows alongside a larger boat and begs for food for himself and his stranded fiancée, but will not go aboard; they have been living on an island covered in a grey fungus that forms 'vast fingers' that reach to the sky. It also creeps towards them with unnerving purpose – and they feel drawn to eating it, even as it begins to grow on them. It's truly a tale of the weird, without meaning or conclusion, choosing to create dread and leave the reader stuck there, thinking through the implications of what has happened for long afterwards.

The Voice in the Night has inspired writers and film-makers all over the world, and perhaps my favourite version is the Japanese horror film *Matango* (1963). After a shipwreck, the castaways end up sheltering on an island that is home to an unpleasant and persistent mould. As it infects them, their behaviour alters; they become aggressive, erratic. Violence erupts, and there is a gruesome discovery to be made. The sound the mushrooms make is memorably horrible: I recommend tracking it down and giving it a listen, in case you ever wanted to know what an angry giant mushroom might sound like. Directed by Ishirō Honda, *Matango* offers social commentary for its times, dealing with nuclear proliferation and addiction.

In the 1980s and 1990s Thomas Ligotti wrote delicate, disturbing short stories, leaving out the shock value to produce a profound sense of disquiet in the reader. Fungi featured wonderfully in his short story *The Shadow at the Bottom of the World* (1991). A scarecrow in a farmer's field moves of its own accord and the locals find it is a fungus, reaching deep into the earth. They try to destroy it and find there is no way to obliterate something that grows so deep, so strong. Soon the community is in fear of it and the way it affects the ground for miles under their town.

From there, the idea of the fungus infecting the world itself rather than just the body – a societal nightmare rather than an individual one – gained traction, as did fear of the small changes, the unseen alterations, that lead to strange, altered environments. Jeff VanderMeer's *Southern Reach Trilogy* was published in 2014 and describes a land in flux; a territory known only as 'Area X' has become uninhabitable, hallucinogenic, deadly to the humans who step inside. There are suggestions of spores in the air, and growths underground – fruiting bodies appear, and begin to write messages to those who dare to trespass. Perhaps this fungus is tired of sharing the world.

M. R. Carey's *The Girl with All the Gifts* (2014) goes further, and suggests that a fungus might use humanity as only one early stage in further development. Using the example of *cordyceps*'s ability to control behaviour, it combines how fungi can affect creatures to its own end with one of the great monstrous creations that has dominated movies and literature for decades – the zombie. Tying both elements together results in a powerful and frightening tale for our times about loss of control and fears of generational conflict.

And now there are fungi from worlds beyond, coming to the page via Tade Thompson's *Rosewater* trilogy. The first novel was published in 2017, and it grips attention with its deft mix of science fiction and adventure, set amid the weirdness of aliens who have released fungal spores in order to make the Earth into the planet they want. Vast environmental upheaval affects many, who ingest the spores and begin the process of becoming more than human. Or is it less than human? Who can tell, except to say that our understanding of what it means to be a singular being, freed from responsibility towards and interconnection with the planet on which we live, has changed massively since Hodgson first wrote of his marooned sailor. Mycological stories are no longer of the mushroom alone, but of the networks to which it – and we – belong.

Perhaps there is only one fear, and that is death. But there are so many ways to die, and to be reborn, created anew. Great stories of fungal fear recognise that it's the alteration that entrances and horrifies us. To be not quite dead, and not quite alive, in any way that we understand. But possibly there are just enough of us left to remember what we were, and to be afraid of what we will become.

7

To Live and Die in Fungi

I t's a hot, windy day in California.

The wind blows through the grapevines and over the famous beaches. It whips down the boulevards of the big cities, snatching at bags and skirts, and it rustles the leaves of the citrus trees. It picks up the arid soil of the fields and forms it into dust clouds, and within the dust is a dangerous, microscopic threat: the desiccated spores of *Cocciodioides immitus*.

A dust cloud in a windstorm can travel for hundreds of miles, and these are adventurous spores, searching hard for a new home. Some of them will find that home in the humans who happen to breathe them in, lodging fast in the lungs. It will cause no pain; the humans won't even be aware of the invasion, at least at first. But time passes, and spores grow.

Once inhaled, the spores become multicellular organisms: spherules. The warm and wet conditions inside the body are good for them, and they develop further, then rupture to form endospores, and the cycle begins again. This process begins to cause damage. If the human host is an unlucky one, symptoms will start to appear: tiredness, a cough, a fever. Shortness of breath. Headaches, muscle aches, night sweats, and maybe a blotchy rash on the upper body or the legs, caused by the inflammation of fat cells under the skin. Pneumonia can develop.

If the host is one of the really unlucky ones, it will spread through the bloodstream, to the bones or brain. This can take years. It can be fatal.

Coccidioidomycosis is also called Valley Fever, and it's not found only in California. The spores are in the soil of many of the south-western US states and beyond into Central and South America. The Centers for Disease Control and Prevention reports that there are roughly

10,000 cases per year in the US alone, but many of them are asymptomatic. Very few progress to cause serious illness. Our bodies, when healthy, are adept at fighting all kinds of foes, including fungi.

Even so, there are times when our bodies need help, and for many of the less serious fungal diseases we face that comes in the form of antifungal medication.

Antifungals can be applied to the skin, swallowed, inserted or injected: clotrimazole, econazole, miconazole. They can ably treat conditions including ringworm, athlete's foot and thrush. It can take time and dedication to beat back a fungal infection, and some can become an opportunistic nightmare if patients have been on long-term antibiotics, or have had their gut mucosa altered. Those suffering with HIV are at extreme risk; half of all fatal diseases in such patients are caused by the fungi *Cryptococcosis* and *Pneumocystosis*.

Research into ways to create an effective fungal vaccine has been conducted for decades: could there really be a way to vaccinate against all such invasions, from *Candida albicans* to *Cocciodioides immitus*? There's no answer to that question yet, but work continues, particularly as understanding grows of the immune system.

Proteomics, the analysis of proteins in cells, might provide solutions, as might the field of DNA vaccination – the injection of an antigen's DNA to give the body instructions on how to fight attackers directly.

But fungi don't always need to be fought.

There's a vast number that can be found as part of what's called the human microbiome: an incredible array of micro-organisms including bacteria and viruses that either colonise us or have formed mutualisms with us or on us, on skin, in hair, in the intestines, say. They can be essential – the human gut, for instance, relies on microbiota. Recent studies have begun to look in more and more detail at the fungal part of this collection of organisms, known as the mycobiome, and their role in maintaining health, suggesting that some forms of gut fungi can even give protection against colitis, or viral infections.

Meanwhile, we live on beside all kinds of fungi, grateful for the ones that aid us, frustrated by the ones that colonise us, and at the mercy of the ones that cannot be stopped. Valley Fever will continue to infect the unlucky and the already ailing. This is what a fungus does. It takes its chances and it spreads, as far and wide as it can, and whenever it finds the right conditions it grows. Not necessarily cool or damp conditions. Any place, any weather you can think of. Even a hot, windy day in California.

Fungi being part of the human world and humans being part of the fungal world: this is an ongoing balancing act. Perhaps we need to learn that we shall always live with fungi. And it has an undeniable role in death too, as a *decomposer* – one of a number of organisms that break down matter, including bacteria and scavengers such as insects. Decomposers feed on decay, process toxins and return essential nutrients to the soil; they are an essential part of the cycle of life and death. The burial industry has traditionally fought against the necessity of decomposition, from ancient mummification techniques to chemical embalming, but things are changing.

The mushroom burial suit or shroud is an idea that is growing in popularity, offering the chance to forgo traditional methods of body disposal that involve the use of chemicals or non-recyclable materials. Instead the deceased is laid to rest in a suit or a cover that has either been seeded with spores or incorporates mycelium so that the breaking down of the body's toxins begins quickly, feeding the fungi and leaving the ground fecund, ready to bear new life. Planting a tree over the place of rest, for instance, results in a lasting, living memorial. Is this the ultimate acceptance of our fungal fate?

8
Grasp

Lithuanian mythology, long lost apart from the barest scraps of stories that survived the Christian onslaught, was filled with gods representing aspects of nature. There were deities for all things: thunder, lightning, trees and rivers. And there was a god, it's said, who had mushrooms for fingers, poking up whenever there were dense, dark woods – an inescapable reminder of death in life. *You'll end up here one day.*

Xylaria polymorpha makes sense of such myths.

Dead Man's Fingers: they rise up from the stumps of a dead beech and clutch at the dank air. They are blackened as if charred from slow fire, gnarled as if they spring from an ancient presence, left long under the ground, forever trying to break through the earth to catch us.

They are still common today but they are not edible. Break one of their black shells open and there's a surprise – a clean white interior, tough and resistant. Find them in any woodland and think of how they must have looked to those who came before, searching the forest for food, and finding themselves in the inescapable presence of a god.

Shakespeare uses this presence in *Hamlet*. When Ophelia's drowned body is found, Queen Gertrude describes her madness that leads to suicide:

> There is a willow grows aslant a brook
> That shows his hoar leaves in the glassy stream;
> There with fantastic garlands did she come
> Of crow-flowers, nettles, daisies, and long purples,
> That liberal shepherds give a grosser name,
> But our cold maids do 'dead men's fingers' call them.
> (*Hamlet*, Act IV, Scene VII)

Ophelia dresses herself in nature to die, and there's no doubt the presence of fungi would fit the theme. But these fingers do not belong to the world of mushrooms.

The name Dead Man's Fingers is too good, perhaps, to be used for only one organism. There's a seaweed that takes the name, and a coral. There's a fruit, and part of a crab. And there's a flower; an orchid, no less. *Orchis mascula* is long and purple. There's some debate, but it's possible that this is what Shakespeare was describing. Orchids, wrapped around the neck of Ophelia: a beautiful, vibrant reminder of life, in bloom, with crowflowers, nettles and daisies for company. Not fungi at all.

Except, as we already know by now, there are no orchids without fungi. Orchids of the family *Orchis* mainly form mycorrhizal relationships with fungi from the *Tulasnellaceae* family, so when we picture the death of Ophelia we are seeing fungi at work whether Gertrude mentions them or not. They are as inescapable as the microfungi floating in the water beside the body, as the mycelia that will eventually slide their way inside after burial, as the decomposition of the body as it travels from young girl to fungal food source.

There's no escaping these fingers. They will, one day, have you in their grasp.

9

Onwards, Downwards, Upwards

This is an end.

It's not the end. It's only one of the five mass extinctions that has happened on Earth. But it is the biggest; up to 95 per cent of all species are lost, over land and in the sea, and entire ecosystems are wiped out. Animals die, plants die. Even trees, en masse, are lost. The ferns and conifers of the Permian Age shrivel and curl up, black and brittle. Entire forests are leafless: nothing living stands. All that is left is the remains of the dead.

But there are fungi.

Fungi, feeding on a feast of rot, erupting and eating and then setting free their spores. The air is thick with them, the smell pervasive. They gorge and swell at intense speed, a riot of beauty born from decay. It's their planet, for a while.

Just when you think it's the end, it turns out to be a beginning.

The Permo-Triassic mass extinction took place 252 million years ago, and the reason for it remains a mystery. Possibly mass volcanic explosions were responsible. Whatever it was, it created an opportunity like no other for fungi to thrive. Their incredibly sudden growth at that time created a record in the sediment of the earth itself. It was a fungal spike like no other, speaking loudly of widespread death once humanity became intelligent enough to listen. Scientists studying the spike have discovered that the extinction came quickly, taking somewhere between 30,000 and 200,000 years; a gradual event would not have produced the same global proliferation.

Fungi are amazing opportunists – that's what the fungal spike after the Permo-Triassic mass extinction teaches us. But we can also see that for ourselves, on a much smaller scale, within the lifetime of human history. From 1348 to 1350 the Black Death killed roughly a third of England's population, and chronicles recorded that, after months of heavy rain, the fields of rotting crops were taken over by enormous, vivid fungi in red, purple and black. What a sight that must have been at a terrifying time. It wouldn't be difficult to assume that these mush-rooms grew equally enthusiastically in the graveyards as in the fields, where there was plenty of extra food to be found. It must have looked like a curse upon the land from God himself.

Much more recently, fungal spikes have been recorded in areas of natural devastation, such as in the wake of volcanic eruptions or forest fires. A fungus was the first organism to be spotted growing healthily on burnt trees after the eruption of Mount St Helens in 1980, for instance.

Although this subject can make many feel repulsed by the immediate ability of some fungi to make the dead their own, I have to admit I find it quite a comforting thought. Nothing is wasted, and there is no end. We're useful and used up, cleanly, efficiently, for the purpose of making more life, more growth, of a form so perfectly suited to this strange planet of carbon expressions. If humanity were to die tomorrow, the fungi would find us, and use us, so that many millions of years later a being might look down into the record of the earth and say, 'There. That's what happened next.'

Afterword

L eaving the far future to itself: here in this present reality, I still have mushrooms on my lawn.

The early-autumn morning has given way to one of those cool afternoons where the sun shines weakly, without the power to warm. Looking out of my bedroom window, I'm aware that the Fairy Ring Champignons will not last long. A few days, at most, and then they'll rot back into the grass. But the mycelial network underneath will continue to grow, sending its messages along the hyphae, interacting with the roots of the plants it finds.

Lawns are boring.

They're designed to be flat, and neat, and to contain only one form of life, if possible. They were the pride of wealthy landowners, from the seventeenth century onwards, because they proved a person had money. They demanded upkeep, and that meant the employment of gardeners who worked hard to stop anything more interesting from sinking its roots into the ground.

The more I look at my lawn, the less sure I am that it serves any purpose in this modern age, when we know that there's no such thing as separation from the land, from nature. No lawn is an island.

There are ways to rewild a lawn. I could leave it unmown, and scatter wild-flower seeds. I could put in a pond for the birds and insects, and plant lavender or buddleia, for the bees. If I wanted to grow my own food and also encourage butterflies, I could put in a patch to grow vegetables, such as brassicas. I've never seen as many caterpillars as I used to find on my father's cabbages; they can strip a plant bare in hours. Maybe I'll accept not getting to eat my produce so much as enjoy watching those bright-green devouring machines at work.

The problem is this: I want to grow more mushrooms. I want patterns of champignons and protuberances of oysters. I want fat field mushrooms and chunky puffballs, and pretty fly agarics: jellies and brackets and boletes. I want a fungal world on my lawn, though it would never fit.

It is possible to grow mushrooms indoors – there are kits to be purchased – or I could even buy some commercial spores, placed within wooden dowels, to be inserted into the right kind of log. I could use waste coffee grounds or use my compost pile. This lawn could be transformed, with a touch of knowledge and a desire to work.

I bought my parents a box of mushrooms to grow at home. There were a range of interesting options, such as pink oysters, *Pleurotus djamor*, but I opted for the classic chestnut – *Agaricus bisporus* with its brown hat on. They sprang readily from the do-it-yourself box that they opened and tended, and they ate the results with interest, and a little trepidation. You never can quite tell with a mushroom.

Suspicions of fungi continue in our family, and the motto *don't touch* still sounds in my head when I'm lucky enough to find brackets or jellies or morels or boletes in my path. That's fine; I'd rather leave them well alone, and let others with expert knowledge and experience do the picking. But I'm glad there are ways to enjoy them without needing to have access to long walks in the few wild places left to us. There are slow-motion films all over social media, taken by those who combine skill and enthusiasm. There are websites and books, and local groups who organise trips, or share precious photos among themselves.

And there is better awareness than ever before of the fact that fungi are all over us, around us, and in us, so this is not a world we can choose to ignore, or escape, because it's their space just as much as it's ours.

I don't have all the answers when it comes to understanding fungi. Few, if any of us, do. But I'm grateful to my father for teaching me to look at them, and to maintain a healthy respect for those things I don't yet understand. And for continuing to teach me that it's OK to be a little afraid, a little entranced, and to peek inside the box.

I look out of my window at my lawn, and at all the lawns along my street, and onwards, through the town, to where the fields and forests lie. Let there be fungi, living their secret lives, for as far as I can see, and beyond. It'll rain soon. I should start work.

Dramatis Fungi

Agaricus bisporus – Common Mushroom (Button, Chestnut, Portobello, Swiss Brown, Italian Brown)

Agaricus campestris – Field Mushroom

Amanita citrina – False Death Cap

Amanita phalloides – Death Cap

Armillaria ostoyae – Humongous Fungus

Ascomycota

Aseroe rubra – Anemone Stinkhorn, Sea Anemone Fungus, Starfish Fungus

Aspergillus tubingensis

Aspergillus versicolor

Cadophora

Caloplaca obamae

Calvatia gigantea – Giant Puffball

Candida albicans

Cladosporium

Claviceps purpurea

Clitocybe rivulosa – Fool's Funnel, False Champignon

Cocciodioides immitus

Coprinellus disseminatus – Fairy Inkcap

Coprinus comatus – Shaggy Inkcap

Cortinarius rubellus – Deadly Webcap

Dictyophora

Fistulina hepatica – Beefsteak Polypore

Fomes fomentarius – Hoof Fungus, Tinder Bracket

Dramatis Fungi

Fomitopsis betulina – Birch Polypore, Razor Strop
Hypholoma fasciculare – Sulphur Tuft
Lepista nuda – Wood Blewit
Loma salmonae
Marasmius oreades – Scotch Bonnet, Fairy Ring Champignon
Mucilago crustacea – Dog Sick Slime Mould
Ophiocordyceps sinensis – Caterpillar Fungus
Ophiocordyceps unilateralis
Oudemansiella mucida – Porcelain Fungus, Poached Egg Fungus
Penicillium citrinum
Penicillium digitatum
Penicillium expansum
Penicillium notatum
Pestalotiopsis microspora
Phallus impudicus – Common Stinkhorn
Phragmidium
Pilobolus crystallinus – Hat Thrower, Dung Cannon
Pleurotus djamor – Pink Oyster
Podostroma cornu-damae – Poison Fire Coral
Psilocybe semilanceata – Liberty Cap, Magic Mushroom
Rachicladosporium africanum
Raffaellea lauricola
Ramalina siliquosa
Rinodina confragosa
Saccharomyces cerevisiae (probably your Sourdough Starter)
Strobilurus tenacellus – Pinecone Cap
Tuber magnatum – White Truffle
Xylaria polymorpha – Dead Man's Fingers

Binomial name not given: Spider Monkey Bile Mushroom (*waña yakino*)

Bibliography

Alenghat, T., W. X. Gladys Ang, T. T. Jiang, J. M. Kinder, G. Pham, T. Shao, L. H. Turner, S. S. Way and J. Whitt, 'Commensal Fungi Recapitulate the Protective Benefits of Intestinal Bacteria', *Cell Host & Microbe*, 22/6 (2017), pp. 809–16. DOI: https://doi.org/10.1016/j.chom.2017.10.013

Ali Shah, A., F. Hasan, S. C. Karunarathna, A. Khan, S. Khan, S. Munir, S. Nadir, Z. Ullah Shah and J. Xu, 'Biodegradation of polyester polyurethane by *Aspergillus tubingensis*', *Environmental Pollution*, 225 (2017), pp. 469–80

Anderson, S, 'The Plastic-Eating Fungi That Could Solve Our Garbage Problem', *Newsweek*, 15 December 2014; retrieved from: https://www.newsweek.com/2014/12/26/plastic-eating-fungi-could-solve-our-garbage-problem-291694.html

BBC Earth Unplugged, 10 October 2013, *Fungus Cannon in Super Slo Motion* [video file]; retrieved from https://youtu.be/T8OAmcUnm4g

BBC News, 8 March 2001, 'Mutant fungus from space'; retrieved from http://news.bbc.co.uk/2/hi/world/monitoring/media_reports/1209034.stm

Berbee, M. L., and T. Y. James, 'No jacket required – new fungal lineage defies dress code', *BioEssays*, 34/2 (2012), pp. 94–102

Bessette, A. E., A. R. Bessette and D. P. Lewis, *Mushrooms of the Gulf Coast States: A Field Guide to Texas, Louisiana, Mississippi, Alabama, and Florida* (Austin: University of Texas Press, 2019)

Bradić, M., 'Towards a Poetics of Weird Biology: Strange Lives of Nonhuman Organisms in Literature', *PULSE: The Journal of Science and Culture*, 6 (2019), pp. 1–22

British Lichen Society Bulletin, 119 (winter 2016); retrieved from https://www.rollrightstones.co.uk/assets/ugc/docs/Lichens-_The_Lichens_of_the_Rollright_Stones_British_Lichen_Society_Bulletin_Winter_2016_web.pdf

Brys, R., H. Jacquemyn, B. Lievens and T. Wiegand, 'Spatial variation in below-ground seed germination and divergent myccorrhizal associations correlate with spatial segregation of three co-occurring orchid species', *Journal of Ecology*, 100 (2012), pp. 1328–37; DOI: 10.1111/j.1365-2745.2012.01998.x

'Can A Rare Hawaiian Mushroom Really Give Women a "Spontaneous Orgasm"?', *Science Alert*, 14 October 2015; retrieved from https://www.sciencealert.com/can-a-rare-hawaiian-mushroom-really-give-women-a-spontaneous-orgasm

Capasso, L., '5,300 years ago, the Ice Man used natural laxatives and antibiotics', *Lancet*, 352/9143 (5 December 1998), p. 1864; DOI: 10.1016/S0140-6736(05)79939-6

Carducci, M. A., M. P. Cosimano, R. R. Griffiths, M. W. Johnson, M. A. Klinedinst, B. D. Richards, W. A. Richards and A. Umbricht, 'Psilocybin produces substantial and sustained decreases in depression and anxiety in patients with life-threatening cancer: A randomized double-blind trial', *Journal of Psychopharmacology*, 30/12 (2016), pp. 1181–97; DOI: 10.1177/0269881116675513

Casadevall, A., and E. Dadachova, 'Ionizing Radiation: how fungi cope, adapt, and exploit with the help of melanin', *Current Opinion in Microbiology*, 11/6 (December 2008), pp. 525–31; DOI: 10.1016/j.mib.2008.09.013

Caughey, G. H., 'The Hereford Fungus Eaters: A Pilgrimage to the Site of the First Fungal Foray', *Fungi*, 11/2 (2018), pp. 6–11

Cavendish, R., 'Death of the Emperor Claudius', *History Today*, 54/10 (October 2004), https://www.historytoday.com/archive/months-past/death-emperor-claudius

Centers for Disease Control and Prevention, *Valley Fever (Coccidioidomycosis)*, 29 August 2019; retrieved from https://www.cdc.gov/fungal/diseases/coccidioidomycosis/index.html

Coeio, *The Infinity Burial Suit* [n.d.]; retrieved from http://coeio.com/

Cortese, D., 'Mycorrhizal fungi: all you need to know about the internet of plants', *The Startup*, 31 December 2019; retrieved from: https://medium.com/swlh/mycorrhizal-fungi-all-you-need-to-know-about-the-internet-of-plants-b217cf505f66

Crous, P. W., E. M. Cruywagen, J. Roux, B. Slippers and M. J. Wingfield, 'Fungi associated with black mould on baobab trees in southern Africa', *Antonie Van Leeuwenhoek*, 108/1 (3 May 2015); DOI: 10.1007/s10482-015-0466-7

Eshet, Y., and M. R. Rampino, 'The fungal and acritarch events as time markers for the latest Permian mass extinction: An update', *Geoscience Frontiers*, 9/1 (January 2018), pp. 147–54

Finger, S., *Origins of Neuroscience: A History of Explorations into Brain Function* (Oxford: Oxford University Press, 2001)

First Nature [n.d.]; retrieved from https://www.first-nature.com/index.php

Ford, Brian. J., 'The Microscope of Linnaeus and His Blind Spot', *The Microscope*, 57/2 (2009), pp. 65–72

Gilbert, O., *The Lichen Hunters* (Sussex: The Book Guild, 2004)

Gonzales Morales, M. R., A. G. Henry, R. C. Power, D. C. Salazar-Garcia and L. G. Straus, 'Microremains from El Mirón Cave human dental calculus suggest a mixed plant–animal subsistence economy during the Magdalenian in Northern Iberia', *Journal of Archaeological Science*, 60 (2015), pp. 39–46

Grünert, H. and R. (1991), *Field Guide to Mushrooms of Britain and Europe* (Ramsbury: The Crowood Press, 1991)

Guinness World Records [n.d.]; retrieved from https://www.guinnessworldrecords.com/

Hebel, D., F. Heisel and K. Schlesier, *Mycotree: Beyond Mining Urban Growth* [n.d.]; retrieved from https://www.mycote.ch/mycotree

Herefordshire Fungus Survey Group; retrieved from: http://herefordfungi.org/index.htm

Herskowitz, I., 'Life Cycle of the Budding Yeast *Saccharomyces cerevisiae*', *Microbiological Reviews*, December 1988, pp. 536–53

Hertsgaard, M., 'Can psychedelics treat climate grief?' *Guardian*, 23 April 2020; retrieved from https://www.theguardian.com/environment/2020/apr/23/can-psychedelics-treat-climate-grief

Hoddle, M., 'Redbay Ambrosia Beetle and Laurel Wilt' [n.d.]; retrieved from https://cisr.ucr.edu/invasive-species/redbay-ambrosia-beetle-and-laurel-wilt

Hulcr, J., and J. Landers, 'The Best Look Yet at the Tiny Fungus Storage Units Inside Ambrosia Beetles', *Entomology Today*, 17 October 2018; retrieved from https://entomologytoday.org/2018/10/17/best-look-yet-tiny-fungus-storage-units-inside-ambrosia-beetles-mycangia/

Hughes, D. P., C. C. Labandeira and T. Wappler, 'Ancient death-grip leaf scars reveal ant–fungal parasitism', *Biology Letters*, 7/1 (23 February 2011), pp. 67–70; DOI: 10.1098/rsbl.2010.0521

Khezripour, K., H. Mirzaei, R. Mohammadi, H. Morovati, S. Nami, and M. Vakili, 'Fungal vaccines, mechanism of actions and immunology: A comprehensive review', *Biomedicine & Pharmacotherapy*, 109 (January 2019), pp. 333–44

Kunzig, R., 'The Biology of . . . Truffles', *Discover*, 1 November 2000; retrieved from https://www.discovermagazine.com/planet-earth/the-biology-of-truffles

Krulwich, R., 'The Rarest Plant in Britain Makes a Ghostly Appearance', *National Geographic* (21 July 2016); retrieved from https://www.nationalgeographic.com/news/2016/07/search-for-rare-british-ghost-orchid/

Lepp, H., 'Aboriginal Use of Fungi', *Australian National Botanic Gardens* (2012); retrieved from http://www.anbg.gov.au/fungi/aboriginal.html

Li-Sun Exotic Mushrooms [n.d.]; retrieved from http://www.li-sunexoticmushrooms.com.au/

Long, L.W., *The Way Through the Woods: Of Mushrooms and Mourning* (London: Scribe UK, 2019)

Lowenhaupt Tsing, A., *The Mushroom at the End of the World* (Princeton: Princeton University Press, 2017)

Marren, P., *Mushrooms: The Natural and Human World of British Fungi* (London: Bloomsbury, 2012)

Money, N. P., *Fungi: A Very Short Introduction* (Oxford: Oxford University Press, 2016)

Mycobank Database [n.d]; retrieved from http://www.mycobank.org/defaultinfo.aspx?Page=Home

Newcomb, T., 'What Does Space Smell Like? Some Say Steak, Some Say Metal', *Time*, 25 July 2012; retrieved from https://newsfeed.time.com/2012/07/25/what-does-space-smell-like-some-say-steak-some-say-metal/

NYC Parks [n.d.], *Central Park: Alice in Wonderland*; retrieved from https://www.nycgovparks.org/parks/central-park/monuments/13

Phillips, R., *Mushrooms* (London: Pan Macmillan, 2006)

Rea, P. A., 'Statins: From Fungus to Pharma', *American Scientist*, September–October 2008; retrieved from https://www.american-scientist.org/article/statins-from-fungus-to-pharma

Rolfe, F. W., and R. T. Rolfe, *The Romance of the Fungus World: An Account of Fungus Life in its Numerous Guises Both Real and Legendary* (Mineola, New York: Dover Publications, 1925)

Rothschild, L., 'Myco-architecture off planet: growing surface structures at destination', *NASA*, 30 March 2018; retrieved from https://www.nasa.gov/directorates/spacetech/niac/2018_Phase_I_Phase_II/Myco-architecture_off_planet/

Rotterzwam [n.d.]; retrieved from https://www.rotterzwam.nl/en_US/

Royal Botanic Gardens Kew, *State of the World's Fungi* (2018); retrieved from https://stateoftheworldsfungi.org/2018/reports/SOTWFungi_2018_Full_Report.pdf

Schmitt, C. L., and M. L. Tatum, *The Malheur National Forest: Location of the World's Largest Living Organism [The Humongous Fungus]*, Pacific Northwest Region: United States Department of Agriculture; retrieved from: https://www.fs.usda.gov/Internet/FSE_DOCUMENTS/fsbdev3_033146.pdf

Schultz, K., 'Demand for "Himalayan Viagra" Fungus Heats Up, Maybe Too Much', *The New York Times*, 27 June 2016, Section A, p. 4

Shang Y., P. Feng and C. Wang, 'Fungi That Infect Insects: Altering Host Behavior and Beyond', *PLoS Pathog*, 11/8 (August 2015); retrieved from https://doi.org/10.1371/journal.ppat.1005037

Shapiro, A., 'Meet Clint Yeastwood and More Hilariously Named Sourdough Starters', *Bon Appetit*, 24 October 2016; retrieved from https://www.bonappetit.com/restaurants-travel/article/ sourdough-starter-names

Spindler, K., *The Man in the Ice* (London: Weidenfeld & Nicolson, 2013)

Stamets, P., *Mycelium Running: How Mushrooms Can Help Save the World* (New York: Ten Speed Press, 2011)

Stone, E., 'Finding Feisty Fungi in Antarctica', *Smithsonian Magazine*, May 2009; retrieved from https://www.smithsonian mag.com/history/finding-feisty-fungi-in-antarctica-124049035/

'Two Years After the Fire, Rotterzwam Opens a New Mushroom Farm', 14 May 2019; retrieved from https://en.rotterdampartners. nl/two-years-after-the-fire-rotterzwam-opens-a-new-mushroom-farm/

UK Fungus Day; retrieved from https://www.ukfungusday.co.uk/

University of California, Riverside, 'New Species of Lichen Named After President Barack Obama', *Science Daily*, 16 April 2009; retrieved from https://www.sciencedaily.com/ releases/2009/04/090415141217.htm

US Food & Drug Administration, *Food Defect Levels Handbook*, 2018; retrieved from https://www.fda.gov/food/ingredients-additives-gras-packaging-guidance-documents-regulatory-information/food-defect-levels-handbook

Wignall, P. B., *Extinction: A Very Short Introduction* (Oxford: Oxford University Press, 2019)

Wohlleben, P., *The Hidden Life of Trees* (London: William Collins, 2017)

World Health Organization [n.d.], *DNA vaccines*; retrieved from https://www.who.int/biologicals/areas/vaccines/dna/en/

Yong, E., 'How the Zombie Fungus Takes Over Ants' Bodies to Control Their Minds', *The Atlantic*, 14 November 2017;

retrieved from https://www.theatlantic.com/science/archive/2017/11/how-the-zombie-fungus-takes-over-ants-bodies-to-control-their-minds/545864/

—, 'Trees That Have Lived for Millennia Are Suddenly Dying', *The Atlantic*, 11 June 2018; retrieved from https://www.theatlantic.com/science/archive/2018/06/baobab-trees-dying-climate-change/562499/?single_page=true

Zent, E., 'Mushrooms for Life among the Jotï in the Venezuelan Guayana', *Economic Botany*, 62/3 (November 2008), pp. 471–81; DOI: 10.1007/s12231-008-9039-2

A Reading List of
Fungal Fiction

Bradbury, R., 'Boys! Raise Giant Mushrooms in Your Cellar!',
   Galaxy Magazine, 1962

Carey, M., *The Girl with All The Gifts* (London: Orbit, 2014)

Devlin, M., 'Her First Harvest', *You Will Grow Into Them* (London:
   Unsung Stories, 2017)

Grey, O., and S. Moreno-Garcia (eds), *Fungi* (Vancouver:
   Innsmouth Free Press, 2012)

Hodgson, W., 'The Voice in the Night', *Blue Book Magazine*,
   1907

Ligotti, T., 'The Shadow at the Bottom of the World', *Grimscribe:
   His Lives and Works* (New York: Carroll & Graf, 1991)

Thompson, T., *Rosewater* (New York: Orbit, 2017)

—, *The Rosewater Insurrection* (New York: Orbit, 2019)

—, *The Rosewater Redemption* (New York: Orbit, 2019)

VanderMeer, J., *Annihilation* (New York: Farrar, Straus and Giroux,
   2014)

—, *Authority* (New York: Farrar, Straus and Giroux, 2014)

—, *Acceptance* (New York: Farrar, Straus and Giroux, 2014)

Weldon, F., *Puffball* (London: Hodder and Stoughton, 1980)

Whiteley, A., *The Beauty* (London: Unsung Stories, 2014)

Wyndham, J., *Trouble with Lichen* (London: Penguin, 1960)

Acknowledgements

During a difficult year for so many of us I was given the opportunity to stick my head into the world of fungi and keep it there, and it has been a wonderful gift for which I have to thank, first and foremost, Simon Spanton. Also many thanks to Sarah Rigby, Pippa Crane, Alison Menzies, and everyone at Elliott & Thompson for making this such a beautiful book.

My first reader, Tim Stretton, gave me courage at the right moment. George Sandison and Neil Ayres kept me moving forward, and Max Edwards handled all the tricky bits of the process with his usual skill and enthusiasm. Thank you to you all.

Nick Whiteley read it and offered the best suggestions, and Elsa Whiteley listed all the dramatis fungi for me. James Ovey made me laugh at all the right points. Nina Allan encouraged me to add more of myself, and she was right, as ever. And thank you, of course, to my parents, who took me on long walks, gave me a camera, and continue to be proud of me as I search out the fascinating things that grow in darkness.

Index